Visitor's
TENE[...]

GW00722463

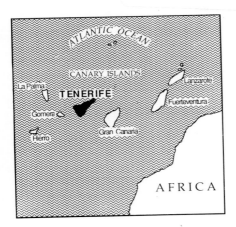

The Author
Rod Weale is an Englishman who lives and works in Tenerife with his
Canarian wife and two sons; they are all interested in and involved with the
island and its people, both the locals and visitors. He has also written a
number of articles on Tenerife which have been published on the island.

VISITOR'S GUIDE
TENERIFE

Rod Weale

MPC
HUNTER

Published by:
Moorland Publishing Co Ltd,
Moor Farm Road West, Ashbourne,
Derbyshire DE6 1HD England

Published in the USA by:
Hunter Publishing Inc,
300 Raritan Center Parkway,CN 94, Edison, NJ 08818

ISBN 0 86190 576 8

British Library Cataloguing in Publication Data:
A catalogue record for this book is available from the British Library

Colour origination by: P. & W. Graphics Pte Ltd, Singapore

Printed in Hong Kong by: Wing King Tong Co Ltd

Cover photograph: International Photobank.
Page 2: The lunar-like landscape of the Teide National Park.
Page 3: A small chapel close to the Parador de Turismo.

Illustrations have been supplied as follows: Spanish National Tourist
Office: pp 51, 59 (bottom), 95, 98 (top), 106 (top), 114; All other illustrations
were supplied by the author.

CONTENTS

Key to Symbols Used in Text Margin and on Maps

🚶	Recommended walk	⛪	Church/Ecclesiastical site
🦌	Nature reserve/Animal interest	⊞	Building of interest
❋	Garden	♜	Castle/Fortification
♣	Parkland	🏛	Museum/Art gallery
⚑	Golf facilities	🏔	Beautiful view/Scenery, Natural phenomenon
※	Other place of interest		

Key to Maps

▬▬▬	Main road	▨	Town/City
═══	Autopista (Motorway)	●	Town/Village
		☁	Lake

How To Use This Guide

This MPC Visitor's Guide has been designed to be as easy to use as possible. Each chapter covers a region or itinerary in a natural progression which gives all the background information to help you enjoy your visit. MPC's distinctive margin symbols, the important places printed in bold, and a comprehensive index enable the reader to find the most interesting places to visit with ease. At the end of each chapter an Additional Information section gives specific details such as addresses and opening times, making this guide a complete sightseeing companion. At the back of the guide the Fact File, arranged in alphabetical order, gives practical information and useful tips to help you plan your holiday — before you go and while you are there. The maps of each region show the main towns, villages, roads and places of interest, but are not designed as route maps and motorists should always use a good recommended road atlas. The routes are intended as a guide and should not necessarily be attempted in one day.

ACKNOWLEDGEMENTS

I would like to express my heartfelt thanks to those who helped and encouraged me in the writing of this book; to Dave and Ros Brawn for the idea and helping along the way; to Carmen, Auggie, Digna, Delia, 'George' and Alan and his family for often accompanying me on my explorations and for tolerating the frequent stops and note-taking sessions; to Peter Warburton and to Richard and Antony for their patience as their father disappeared around the island and then to his study. Last but not least, I would like to thank Tenerife, for sharing her beauty and her people and for making myself and all others welcome.

I would also like to dedicate this book to my parents.

Rod Weale
Chiguergue, Guia de Isora

FOREWORD

In the research for this book I travelled and explored every tarmac road on this island and many of the dirt tracks. In all I drove well in excess of 2,000km. At no time was I bored, this island is a truly fascinating place. In a few thousand square kilometres Tenerife has so much to see and enjoy including deserts, mountains, sand and sea. The climate is idyllic and the people are friendly. Having explored the island, I have discovered my favourite places just as you will discover yours. It may be a beach, sheltered from winds and undiscovered by tourism, a wood where you can listen to the breeze in the trees and the songs of the birds. You may find peace in the remote villages of the interior and enjoy the company of the locals as they, like you, relax with beer in hand.

To appreciate Tenerife to the full you need to travel her highways and byways. There are a number of ways to get about the island but the most convenient and often least expensive is by hire car. In my research I considered that the traveller would be driving the smallest, most basic and most popular car available for hire — a Seat Panda/Marbella. Many hire companies now have replaced these cars with Opel Corsa, Renault Clio and similar size cars. In the rare instances where four wheel drive vehicles are essential, it has been indicated.

Hopefully the visit to Tenerife will be voted a success and further visits planned. This island, given the chance, can tempt, bewitch and capture the heart of the most experienced traveller. It will offer a variety of sights, sounds and tradition that few other holiday destinations can match, everything from sun and sea to snow and sand. Tenerife can be barren but never boring, arid but also alluring, at times untidy but never uninteresting. The island has a charm that entices even the most travelled visitor to return time and time again.

INTRODUCTION

History

Tenerife is one of the Fortunate Islands, subject of a thousand legends and an island that, contrary to popular belief, has a history that pre-dates the building of the first hotel. The story of the Canary Islands is spiced with mystical tales that remain the subject of scholarly discussion today. The gardens of Hesperides where Mount Atlas climbed to the heavens are said to have been here. Many still believe that the Canaries are the remains of the lost continent of Atlantis.

To understand and appreciate Tenerife to the full, one should understand something of its history. There is some debate as to how the indiginous aboriginal people that the first explorers discovered on their arrival came to inhabit the islands. Such is the complexity of the theories that have been put forward that it would be impossible to include all of them. Historians, anthropologists, archaeologists, botanists, geologists and astronomers have come and gone to leave a wealth of theories about every aspect of the island's evolution.

Plato wrote of Atlantis and since then others have added or detracted from his suppositions. Ancient Roman and Greek writers told of Fortunate or Blessed Islands to the west of their known world. It is unclear when exactly the civilised world 'discovered' the Canaries. It is certain that merchants, in the quest for new goods to lay before the nobles of Europe, visited the islands in the early Middle Ages and were left with a wondrous impression.

On their return to the courts of Europe, the merchants described the people that inhabited the islands as a peaceful, handsome race but one that was comparatively uncivilised. The European visitors found people that still dressed in animal hide, lived in caves and

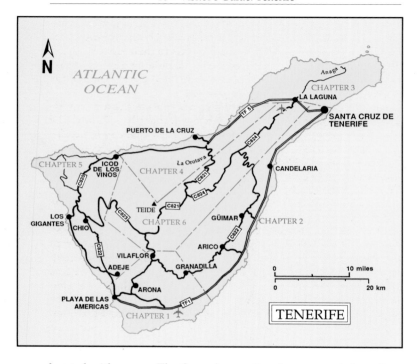

hunted with spears. The Guanches, as they have come to be collectively known, were tall, blond and had blue eyes. (Guanche is the ancient word for 'man' in the original language of Tenerife. It has been adopted to mean all the ancient inhabitants of the Canaries). This has given rise to speculation about their origins. Their physical characteristics suggest that they originated in Scandinavia while others argue that their art of mummifying their dead indicates an Egyptian heritage. Both theories rely on the fact that the two civilisations concerned were great mariners and explorers and had the craft to sail forth from their homelands to make landfall in the Canary Islands. If the Guanches arrived by sea they soon forgot their heritage — early visitors to the islands found a race that possessed little knowledge of navigation and had little contact with the other islands in the archipelago.

If the islands were known to the great European powers of the Middle Ages, one wonders why no attempt to colonise the islands was made. The nearest seafaring nations were Portugal and Spain, both of whom knew of the islands' existence and apparent abundance. Up to the fifteenth century the crowns of both countries were fragile and, despite the desire to add lands to their kingdoms, the defence of their 'home front' was understandably given priority. Indeed, when the crown of Castile commenced the invasion of the islands, Spain was still a divided country.

The 'invasion' started in 1402 when the Norman Baron Jean de Béthencort stepped ashore in Lanzarote to a friendly welcome. The conquest of the Canary Islands was to occupy Spanish forces for most of the fifteenth century. It was not so markedly bloody and violent as later Spanish campaigns in the New World, but there were several bloody defeats inflicted on the modern Spanish armies by the Guanches who fought with little more than sticks and stones.

The islands fell to a now united Spain one by one, Tenerife was the last to be conquered. Having bypassed the biggest and most powerful island as the conquest continued, the Spanish eventually landed on the beach at Anaga, near the site of today's capital. From the first landing on 1 May 1494, the fate of Tenerife was sealed. However, while the Spanish were better equipped with resources and equipment few European nations could match, they were confronted by a people determined to fight for their land. Béthencourt had died in 1425 and the subsequent Spanish conquests had been undertaken by a number of generals. Alonso de Lugo had subdued La Palma before leading his troops to Tenerife.

Tenerife was politically divided into a number of smaller 'kingdoms' controlled by Menceys, princes who now joined to fight the invader. Not all rallied to the cause and the Mencey of Tacoronte allied his troops to the Spanish and was to prove a valuable source of information and a faithful ally. The Spanish drove inland and had got to Orotava without forcing the Guanches to battle. Like their modernday counterparts, the Spanish were discovering the difficulties of fighting an army that knows the land and is practised in the art of 'guerilla' tactics. The Guanches withdrew, the Spanish followed and the trap was sprung. In the Battle of Acentejo on 31 May 1494, the Spanish suffered a defeat that put them to flight and back to their encampment at Anaga. Reinforced, the Spanish marched into the interior again and the experiences of the previous spring were well heeded. On 14 November 1494 a pitched battle took place near La Laguna and this time the Spanish inflicted a crushing defeat upon the natives. Consolidating their position, the Spanish followed this victory with another at the site of their previous defeat. Today the village of La Victoria (The Victory) is near the site of the battle.

The Guanches that survived the battles fled to the hills and never reunited in sufficient strength to meet the invaders in force again. As the Spanish advanced, Bencomo the Guanche leader saw the chances of success diminish and surrendered. By September 1496 the island was subdued and the Spanish ruled all the Canary Islands. The conquest was later ratified by the Pope and Portugal, who had earlier laid claims on the islands, accepted the Spanish right of rule.

In 1492 Christopher Columbus had visited the islands on his way west. According to legend, he recruited men from the subdued islands and the sailor who first spied the New World was a Guanche; perhaps this story was invented to illustrate the new found alliance. Despite the fact that the Spanish had taken their islands for their own, the Guanches accepted Spanish rule with little hesitancy. In return, the Spanish offered the benefits of a modern society, freedom from slavery and rights to land. It has to be noted that the Guanches fared better than the Incas and Aztecs of South America and that their integration was, by contemporary standards, a peaceful one.

As the Spanish headed west so did the natives. Today the ties with South America are perhaps stronger here than in the mainland. In almost every country you will find places and areas that take their name from their Canarian heritage. Today many families have close ties with Cuba and Venezuela in particular. The Spanish conquerers soon became settlers, the rich fertile soil was first used for the production of sugar and later vines. A firm but fair rule meant the islanders soon saw themselves as one, an independent feeling that exists today. The Spanish might in the following centuries was mainly due to the wealth of the New World. The galleons that sailed west to return laden with gold and jewels used the ports of The Canaries as victualling stops. The history in modern times tells of Nelson's ill-fated attack on Santa Cruz, an attack with cost him his arm as well as his pride. Francisco Franco was military governor of the islands and it was in Tenerife that he hatched the plan that led Spain into the bloody Civil War.

Having been given the status of being duty free by Royal Decree in the nineteenth century, trade in the islands flourished. They became an important trade centre and the ports of Santa Cruz in Tenerife and Las Palmas in Gran Canaria became two of the busiest ports in the world. Even though they are no longer duty free, the islands do enjoy low import taxes and the two ports are always busy. Just as the Spanish galleons used the islands, they are a frequent port of call for modern fleets. It is possible to see Russian trawlers tied alongside navy frigates, container vessels and car ferries.

In 1927 the islands were divided into two provinces; Santa Cruz de Tenerife oversees the western islands of Tenerife, Gomera, El Hierro and La Palma, whereas Las Palma de Gran Canaria plays host to the parliament that governs Gran Canaria, Lanzarote and Fuerteventura. With the monarchy restored to Spain in 1975, these parliaments became democratic and while the islands are still ultimately governed by Spain, they enjoy a considerable amount of autonomy.

Visit the Canary Islands today and the evidence of the boom years enjoyed in the 1960s and 1970s is obvious. Today it is tourism that provides the majority of the island's income. Every year millions of people discover the Fortunate Islands and enjoy a climate that the world envies. Perhaps the mystery of how these islands came to be will never be solved but their magic and wonder is there for all to enjoy.

Geography

An island of contrast is a simple but nevertheless accurate way of describing Tenerife. The island is the largest of the seven main islands that form the Canarian archipelago. It is now generally accepted that the name Canary comes from the fact that early visitors to Gran Canaria discovered large dogs on the islands, the latin for dog being *canis*. Tenerife was called *Nivaria* in ancient times after the snowcapped mountain. The mountain that towers over the island was *tener* (mountain) *if* (white) to the Gomeran islanders, and so the island became Tenerife to later visitors.

The peak of Teide that rises from the centre of the island is the landmark for which Tenerife is best known, at 3,717m (12,200ft) it is the highest mountain on Spanish territory. It is often snowcapped and yet, at most, is 90 minutes from a beach. The contrast continues on the journey between the coast and the mountain, this variety in landscape, flora and fauna is exaggerated further in the contrast between the geographic areas of the island.

The island is basically triangular in shape. The base runs southwest to north-east. At the eastern end, the two coasts, 'north' and 'south' then run east to converge in a 'point' east of the capital Santa Cruz. The island's geological heritage is the subject of speculation. The mountain ranges at the western and eastern tips give rise to the belief that at one time there were two separate islands later joined by the volcanic activity of the sea that divided them. The volcanic ancestry is there for all to see and many esteemed geologists maintain that this disproves the theory that these islands were once part of a gigantic continent that linked Africa and the Americas. The nearby African coast shows no sign of ancient volcanic activity. Regardless of the facts and theories, myths and stories that surround the island's heritage, the legacy is a wonderland of contrast wherever one looks. The tourist boom has seen resorts spring from desert, improvements in the facilities inland and all the infrastructure to cope with the demand of the visitor. Despite the fact that tourism has made a permanent impression, it cannot be considered to have completely taken over the island. Although the industry has a great influence on all aspects of island life, it touches very little of the island's surface. There are four main tourist areas, Playa de las Americas, including Los Cristianos (they can no longer be considered separately), Puerto de la Cruz, Los Gigantes and the Costa del Silencio. At regular intervals around the coast are smaller 'resorts' such as San Marcos, El Medano, Callao Salvaje and Playa de la Arena.

Away from the resorts there lies an island that remains relatively untouched by the travel industry. That is not to say it is ignorant of it, the international signs that adorn many restaurants bear witness to that. The interior of the island, together with the untouched and often very accessible coast, are the real Tenerife. Away from the neon and the noise of the resorts and towns is a wealth and variety of untouched beauty that few visitors can wait to return to.

Plant and Animal Life

The sub-tropical temperature that Tenerife enjoys has ensured that the plant life that can be seen on the island is as varied as one could find anywhere in the world. Many of the plants that adorn the slopes and valleys of the mountain are indigenous, whereas others have been 'imported', some from as far away as Australasia and South America. Such is the variety, that it would prove impossible to list and make comment on all the species and sub-species that grow here. Accordingly, those plants that are of particular interest are referred to in the text where it is appropriate.

The plants can be divided into definite sections. Firstly there are those that are grown not for their beauty but their produce. Bananas, vines, potatoes, almonds and figs are to be found in abundance throughout the island. Less common plants such as papaya and avocado add further colour. The flowering trees, shrubs and plants add background colour to the landscape. Some grow wild and have been left to spread their colour along the lanes, roads and in the gardens. The cactus that seems to take any available space is still cultivated for commercial reasons in some areas but in general the cacti grow wild and unattended.

The centre of the island is high and rocky due to volcanic activity

Woodlands spring up from the bare rock

Despite the advance of the tourist industry, agriculture still remains a principal source of income on Tenerife, as well as employing a large number of people. When the Spanish had conquered the island and began to change from conquerors to settlers, they grew sugar cane in enormous quantities. The boom that this brought the island was short lived, as the new world opened it became cheaper to produce sugar in the Indies and accordingly the industry declined. The 'new' crop of potatoes was introduced and today remains an important crop, albeit mainly to satisfy the island's own needs. However, it is for the tomato and banana that the Canarian Islands are best known. The climate ensures that the crops are ripe when the demand is greatest and the produce is exported worldwide.

Agriculture still utilises by far the greatest proportion of the island's usable land. As you travel to the more remote parts of Tenerife you realise just how large a percentage of the islands land has been cultivated. Today the evidence of the decline in agriculture is everywhere; the deserted terraces and *fincas*, their walls built by hand, are now crumbling as the land slowly returns to nature. Farming in many parts of Tenerife is hard, the volcanic eruptions left steep gradients that have had to be terraced. The soil in many of the *fincas* has been 'imported' and is retained by the walls, protected from the harsh, eroding winds.

Water is surprisingly plentiful in Tenerife, the problem facing the farmer has been to provide his crops with a regular and pure supply. The canals and pipes that scar the landscape feed the *fincas* from the sources in the hills, an intricate system tailored to satisfy the thirst of crops growing in the arid soil. There is a marked difference between the farms and collectives found in the different areas of Tenerife. The geological and meteorological differences between north and south, often dictated by the mountain, ensure that a great variety of crops are grown throughout the island.

In the lush north one is more likely to find the crops that flourish in the moist soil and are not sensitive to extreme heat. In the south the tomato and banana plantations can be seen everywhere, often protected from the sun in plastic houses where the lights at night create a permanent 'sun'. As tourism has taken a grip in the south, those who toil the land often do not follow their fathers and grandfathers. The lure of a guaranteed wage without the often arduous work associated with agriculture has seen many desert to the resorts. However, some remain, growing the crops to be collected for market or to be packed for export in the many co-operatives.

Flowers are not only ever-present at the roadside but remain an to be found in the florists of Europe, the climate here ensuring that supplies are constant throughout the year. Flowers and flowering shrubs that one sees in Europe as pot plants grow freely here at the roadside and in the parks and villages. Poinsettia, hibiscus and others thrive in a splendid array of colour, and almond trees in blossom add their distinct colour. Such is the climate of the island that some of these plants grow to a huge size and the array and brightness of the colours are breathtaking. Enthusiasts should visit the Botanical Gardens in Puerto de la Cruz, one of the foremost botanical centres in the world.

Tenerife is not renowned for its animal life. The harsh climate has meant that only the most hardy and adaptive animals have survived. In the forests and among the flora of the *barranco* (deep valley), rabbit and hare are widespread and are hunted for food. Higher, away from the coast, birds of prey can be seen circling on the thermals as they scan the rocks and plants below for food. The lizard provides much of their diet. Many species abound in the islands, some are as long as 25cm (10in). They are all harmless, despite their prehistoric appearance. The Canary bird is to be found in the forested areas, being difficult to spot, they are more often to be heard. It is interesting to note that only the male sings and that the bird will, in captivity, change from a sparrow-like colour to the familiar 'yellow'. A favourite sport amongst the village boys is to set traps for this elusive bird.

Marine life abounds off the coasts of Tenerife. Dolphins can often be seen from the shore, playing in the surf, while sharks and whales are not common but do visit the waters further away from the shore. Fish of all shapes, sizes and tastes swim in the warm waters and, not surprisingly, are fished on a large scale. Marlin now visit the shores and provide an exciting challenge to fishermen.

Many of the resorts are also fishing ports and the restaurants take full advantage of this plentiful and inexpensive source of fare. As you travel around the coast you will often see amateur fishermen casting from the rocks, in many coastal villages fish is the staple diet.

Climate

It is the excellent climate that the Canary Islands enjoy that has seen the tourist industry take such an important place in Tenerife's economy and way of life. The climatic conditions are inevitably influenced by the height and position of Teide. The phrase 'eternal spring' is often used to illustrate the temperate climate the islands enjoy. The temperature rarely rises above 25°C (78°F) and rarely falls below 16°C (64°F). As you climb higher the temperature falls

Las Terisitas is one of the beaches in Tenerife which has imported golden sand

Spread across the island are fincas — small cultivated plots of land

and on top of Teide it is often well below freezing. Even in summer there is moisture to be found above the coastal plains but Tenerife is not a rainy island and one is likely to encounter only a days rain per month in spring and autumn. The monsoon-like showers are heavy but brief and unlikely to spoil your day out. In winter the mountain will often be covered in snow and, despite the brilliant sunshine, it will be bitterly cold on top of Teide. The roads of Tenerife have little drainage and you will often encounter rocks and mud washed onto the road by the rivulets that form. It is just a question of using common sense when driving in these conditions.

Food and Drink

Tenerife is something of a gourmet's delight and yet, surprisingly, the island is not renowned for its food. The resorts offer the traditional English breakfasts and the hamburger bars. You will find some excellent restaurants, offering typical fare but, away from the resorts there are numerous restaurants where you will find first class food and tapas, often at a very reasonable cost.

All types of meat abound; pork, chicken and beef are to be found everywhere and veal, rabbit and lamb are common. Depending on your own preference, you can have these with chips or enjoy a sauce with Canarian Potatoes. These are boiled in their skins and are salty and extremely tasty. Mojo will be offered, this is a garlic dressing which brings out the flavour of the meat but try a bit first as some are very hot.

Fish is an important part of the Canarian diet. Almost without exception the fish restaurants are to be found in the ports and resorts. There are many species, some of which may not be familiar, many restaurants will advise you on a suitable fish if you ask, white meat, filleted etc. Most are served *a la planca* (shallow fried) and sauces are optional.

Tapas bars are to be found all over Tenerife, many are no more than village bars that offer a variety of snacks. Octopus, squid, salads and meat in sauces are common and can provide a filling snack. Most dishes are prepared daily so are fresh and the standard of cooking is high. In addition, a *pepito* can fill the gap. This is a bread bun filled with slices of steak or pork with salad filling. Spanish omelette is also common and comes in a variety of shapes and sizes.

For cooking in your apartment a visit to the supermarket will provide you with most things you need. If there is a butcher (*carniceria*) locally then fresh meat and sometimes fish are freely available.

Many restaurants outside the resorts may not present a menu, the waiter will simply list what is available. You may also find meat priced per kilo, make sure that you ask the price first. Most restaurants offer plain, good and cheap fare but if you are in doubt about the price you should ask. Away from the resorts, sweets and desserts may be limited to ice-cream or cakes. Some restaurants offer fresh fruits or cream caramels, usually a menu for sweets will be presented.

Tenerife is a hot, often arid island and a refreshing drink is often welcome. Beer is freely available everywhere, the local brewery is C.C.C., known to many people just as Dorada. This lager-beer is presented in two strengths, you will usually find the normal and 'Gold Top' the most popular. It is available in many places on draught but in villages usually only bottles are available. English style bitter is imported and found only in the resorts. In addition, other Canarians brands and the famous San Miguel are available. Spirits are served in large measures and all best-known types are freely available, even if your favourite brand name may not be. Non-alcholic drinks such as coke, lemonade and orangeade are all available in bottles and cans.

Coffee is served fresh and often strong, white coffee or black are available and a *cortado* makes a pleasant change. This is a small coffee with condensed milk and, if asked for, natural milk as well. It is quite sweet and surprisingly refreshing. Tea is available but is often served without milk.

The water in Tenerife varies in quality. A good general rule is not to drink tap water although in the hills it can be very pure. Bottled water is best and available in restaurants and supermarkets. If you are drinking in a local bar you may not be charged for water if you are in a party or are simply having a 'chaser' after another drink.

Special diets, such as vegetarian have become more catered for but restaurants will often provide for special needs on request. Vegetables are abundant and the Canarians have many ways of presenting non-meat and fish dishes. In addition, children are welcome and restaurants are usually happy to cook a snack for them.

Dining out in Tenerife can be cheap and very satisfying, eating houses are clean and service quick and polite. In the interior of the island choice may be limited but the food remains often better value than the resort restaurants. Drink is available all day and prices compare favourably to the rest of Europe.

Local Events and Festivals

The religious significance of many of the fiestas and festivals may be lost on many visitors but they remain an important part of the island's religious beliefs. Accordingly, while you will be welcome at the events, you should consider their relevance and act accordingly.

Most villages have two saints, one male and one female, each of which is the patron saint of a fiesta. Most religious fiestas take place between February and September, in addition many of the ports will have an extra fiesta, on the day of the fishermen for example.

Carnival is the biggest event of the year on the island. It takes place in February and Santa Cruz plays host to many hundreds of thousands of guests, groups and bands. From there carnival goes to the resorts and larger towns. The nights belong to the beat of salsa and dancing continues into the very early hours. The religious ceremonies include services in churches and the burning of the sardine which signifies the end of the carnival. This 'fish' is carried to its pyre where it is set on fire amongst much ceremony.

Fiestas in local villages are very much a local event, the plaza or square is decorated and various events are centred around here. On Saturday night or Sunday morning the saints of the village are paraded around the streets, while the young men of the village set off rockets to clear the path of demons. These processions are very private and solemn. You will be welcome but keeping a low profile will be appreciated. In the evening there is a dance to a live orchestra and the sound of salsa abounds. Many large towns have a bank holiday around their fiesta, while shops and banks will close here, in the next town life will go on as normal.

Corpus Cristi is celebrated all over the island but the major events are in La Orotava and La Laguna where the streets are laid with carpets of flowers. For the week preceding the festival the locals lay the flowers to the intricate designs laid on the road, the colourful result is well worth a visit.

July 25 is a national holiday. The patron saint of Spain is Santiago Apostel (St James). In Candelaria the virgin is paraded and there are folk dances and offerings of flowers and produce. The virgin on this day is a glorious sight; dressed in her finest robes and adorned with gold she stands outside the basilica while the celebrations go on. In Santa Cruz the day is also celebrated, on this day they recall the defeat inflicted on Nelson and the British fleet.

The remaining 'bank holidays' are celebrated in a more restrained manner and you may find events that only take place in the capital and larger towns.

1
SOUTHERN TENERIFE

The southern part of the island is the most popular with the tourist industry. The resorts of Playa de Las Americas, Los Gigantes and the Costa del Silencio cater for millions of visitors each year. West of the airport the tourist industry is always in evidence. To the east and along the *autopista* the industry is less evident, but a small resort is occasionally seen amongst the sand-coloured wilderness. The south is an arid area. While Los Cristianos can claim a history of fishing, Las Americas is a purpose-built resort and the only evidence of the former character of the land on which the resort stands is the gradient that leads away from the coast.

The desert-like character that dominates the lands east of Las Americas contrasts with the area just inland. At Adeje the hills that form a backdrop to the town and surrounding area are spectacular. Through to Guia de Isora and on the coast road to Los Gigantes areas of the desert have been transformed into rich plantations where bananas are grown and tomatoes stand protected from the wind by rustic fences or modern greenhouses. Fishing ports, deserted beaches, busy resorts, mountains and a wealth of colour, that is the south.

❋   Had you arrived in **Playa de las Americas** a little more than 20 years ago you would have found a few hotels built near the beach, made golden by the imported sands of the Sahara. Even at the start of the 1980s the areas that now house the high class hotels to the east of the original resort and the hills of San Eugenio were little more than barren, arid desert. Las Americas is a resort created for pleasure. Visitors are offered numerous opportunities to indulge themselves and restaurants can be found every few metres. Bars offer English videos while you drink English beer. Daytime pursuits around the

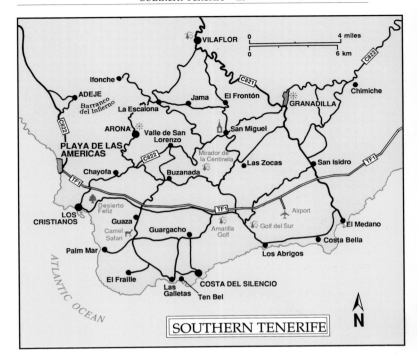

SOUTHERN TENERIFE

busy beaches include waterskiing, boat trips and sky riding, all of which you are encouraged to enjoy by an army of canvassers. One of the first developments in San Eugenio was the Aguapark or Octopus Park. Open all year round, the park offers fun for all the family and young and old can brave the famous water-slides. The beaches are well maintained but are often crowded.

The newer parts of the resort have been built incorporating the lessons from the earlier areas. They have wider roads, are tree-lined and have wider pavements. The buildings are larger but not as high as their predecessors and are of a more varied design, giving an often pleasing skyline. The new marina at Puerto Colon has an air of escapism about it. The rich show off their vessels here and relax in the pavement bars telling of other days in other ports. Further west Fañabe has become a resort. This area could become one of the most desirable resorts in Europe.

The road system in Las Americas is best described as chaotic. Now the southern *autopista* has at last been extended to the resort but the fact remains that with one main road bisecting the resort and an ever busy entry and exit scheme that is always busy, driving in Las Americas is far from straightforward. With the building of the *autopista* this may well change, but for easier access and exit the Arona/Los Cristianos interchange is to be recommended. The junction is busy but, having been redesigned and rebuilt in 1988, it is practical and easy to use.

Leaving the *autopista* the road divides. The right hand lane will allow you to bypass Los Cristianos and head towards Las Americas. Turning right at the roundabout adorned with an unusual piece of modern sculpture and following the road to the T junction will bring you out almost opposite the main beaches. Turn right here and the beaches are on your left. By continuing in the left hand lane you approach Los Cristianos. The centre of the village is best approached by following the road to the large, traffic light controlled, cross roads. Turn right then left. The road leads to the plaza. It may be here that you first come across the parking meter system.

If you park anywhere in Tenerife where the parking lines are blue you should display a ticket. Machines are signposted by a large rectangular sign with a coin being held in fingers. The costs vary as do the times when you should pay. Read the meter, there is normally an English version of the instructions. If you overstay or do not display a ticket you can pay an instant fine, often 150 ptas., by putting the fine ticket in the machine and paying the fine.

If you turn left at the T junction you pass the shopping malls and continue on towards the hotel at the southern end of the resort, where turning right in front of the Hotel Conquisator brings you down to a quiet beach where shelter from the wind can often be found in the dunes. The centre of Las Americas is best seen on foot. Parking is often difficult but if you take one of the many turnings off the beach road you may find a space.

❊   **Los Cristianos** was once a small fishing village but it too has spread out and up. Hemmed in only by the Guaza mountain, the town has now joined Playa de las Americas in everything but name. Even so, Los Cristianos has retained a great many of the traditional features of the original fishing village. The ferries to La Gomera leave from the port and the ticket office is near the berths.

On leaving the autopista and heading towards the town, it is best to follow the signs to the port (*muele*). By doing so you avoid the cramped roads of the town centre. As the dual carriageway ends, take the left hand lane and follow it around to the right. There is an excellent and often uncrowded beach below the car park you see on your right but even if you are not here to swim or take in the sun, parking here will leave only a short walk into the centre. The pedestrianised area has good restaurants and shops. Many of the streets are designed to help the disabled and there are plenty of ramps. Below the main avenue 'Avenida de Suecia' are the narrow walkways that lead to the sea. Families remain in residence here, living in traditional houses.

The main beach at Los Cristianos is busy but it is a large expanse of imported sand that has enough room for everyone. The sand is fine and clean and the water is shallow which makes it ideal for children. Sunbeds and parasols can be hired and there is a manned first aid post on the beach. In front is the busy port and behind this the walkways and bars provide plenty to see and do. There are few hotels in Los Cristianos as most of the buildings are private apartments. Recently the building has increased as land on the slopes at the back of the resort has been released for development.

Las Americas and Los Cristianos have earned a great deal of criticism in the past both being branded as concrete jungles and overcrowded with loud music, but whether this is justified or not, the fact remains that they satisfy the needs of many visitors. The hustle and bustle can be avoided even in the centres, and away from the neon and noise quiet traditional bars and restaurants can be found. There is something for everyone.

It is surprising how little distance one needs to travel away from the resorts before leaving the fast lane behind. The road that leads away from Los Cristianos and into the hills is frequently used for the trip to Teide. The region is rich with sights and tradition that few have discovered.

At the Los Cristianos junction of the motorway, follow the signs to Arona. The road surface here is excellent, and occasionally visible alongside are the remains of the old road — overgrown and awaiting the bulldozer. Our road climbs quickly and 3km (2 miles) from the *autopista* you enter the small village of **Chayofa**. This sleepy hamlet has recently woken up and exclusive villas are being built. The large laurel bushes secure privacy for those fortunate enough to live here and they also provide an attractive feature for those just passing through. As the road leaves Chayofa the climb becomes steeper.

A kilometre (½ mile) beyond Chayofa, just before you enter La Camella, the road to Teide is on your left and well signposted. As you continue to climb the terrain becomes featureless and arid, and the sand-coloured rock is pitted and sun-baked. Spare time to look over

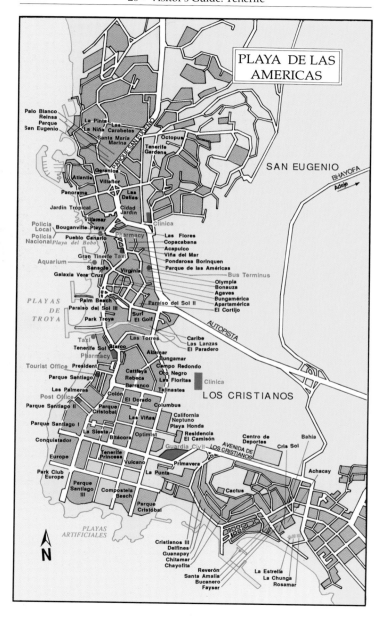

The new marina at Puerto Colon

The beach at Playa de las Americas with a backcloth of barren mountains

your shoulder, for as you climb the views down into the resorts below are splendid. At 8km (5 miles) the important town of **Arona** is seen. Although you are told to turn left just before entering the town if you are travelling further, it is worth carrying on into Arona. This is one of the most important and wealthiest towns in the Canaries. From here Los Cristianos and a big part of Las Americas is governed.

In common with many important towns, Arona feels obliged to have a one way system, although some of the streets are so narrow that one of two passing donkeys would have to give way. The system is easy to follow and by doing so you will reach the top of the town and the plaza. The Ayuntamiento (Town Hall) is here, as is the church, and there are bars where refreshment can be taken. Arona has a small number of shops that are well worth exploring. Prices will compare favourably with those of the resorts. There are also banks, petrol stations and a post office. Try and find time to walk through the narrow streets where the architecture, although not spectacular, is traditional and each street has great character.

Leaving Arona on the road to Teide, you still climb and will continue to do so for some time. Here there is evidence of agriculture. The terraces painstakingly built by hand have often been reclaimed by nature. Only occasionally will you see a terrace that is still farmed. Almond trees cling to the side of deep valleys (*barrancos*), roots are often visible in the eroded earth as they search for water in the dry soil. The road surface remains good and within 6km (4 miles) of Arona you enter the town of La Escalona. If you have time take the turning to **Ifonche**. You will have to come back as it is a dead end but this widespread village is worth visiting. The church on the left stands alone among the *fincas* (plots of land). Follow the road a few kilometres and drive down and around a beautiful *barranco* and to the end of the road. The tarmac track is replaced by a dirt lane that should be negotiated with care. Those feeling energetic can walk to the famous Barranco del Infierno.

From La Escalona you can head down or continue upwards. At the end of the wide, straight avenue around which the town is built is a right hand turn signposted to San Miguel. This road drops rapidly and provides excellent views of the coastal plain below. After 3km (2 miles) the village of Jama can be found on the left. Turn up off the main road and you will find a quaint church nestling amongst the typical houses. Below lies San Miguel.

As you continue upwards from La Escalona towards Vilaflor and for 6½km (4 miles), you will see that the land is bare except for the occasional vine but it is the view to the front that is more memorable.

Vilaflor is the highest parish in Tenerife. At a height of 1,400m (4,600ft), this charming town sits below the National Park among some of the most beautiful scenery to be found on the island. Indeed, Vilaflor itself is not unattractive. As you reach the T junction, turn left and on your left you will see signs for the *mirador* or viewpoint, from which you can look over the town and beyond to the coast. There are a number of restaurants in the town. As with Arona it is worth parking to view on foot the church and houses. The area beyond Vilaflor is described along with Teide in Chapter 6.

If you turn right at the T junction the road will lead you down to the important and busy town of **Granadilla**. It is home to the local courts and is a busy, bureaucratic town. It has a charming colonial feel and an excellent variety of shops. Just as you leave the last house behind there is a small turning on your right signposted San Miguel. This road appears on few maps and yet is a rewardingly scenic route that offers a great deal to see. The 10km (6 miles) take you through a spectrum of views and colours, everywhere there is something to note; such as sandy terraces where figs, almonds and vines grow; and stone walls and bridges that stand in tribute to the skill and endeavour of the local farmers. As you drop down, look back at the views of Teide and Las Canadas, then left to the views across the valley. At this altitude the first of the pine trees appear, and the higher you are the more in evidence these valuable trees become. The village of El Frontón is small and widespread, and you may only realise it was there at all when you reach the T junction and the village is signposted.

Turn right here and you soon reach **San Miguel**. This busy town seems to provide all the support industry for the coast, such as furniture centres, car sales, warehouses and a variety of restaurants. It is best viewed from below the main road. There is a pretty church and a variety of shops. Carry on west from San Miguel and before Valle San Lorenzo stop at the Mirador de la Centeniela which provides excellent views of the surrounding countryside. Beyond the *mirador* lies Valle San Lorenzo and beyond that La Camella and Chayofa. Go east from San Miguel and the main road leads to Granadilla.

There are two roads that will lead you to the coast from here. The quickest route is to follow the road directly to San Isidro. However, if your destination is Las Americas, turn left 2km (1 mile) from Granadilla and follow the road to Las Socas. After 4km (2½ miles) there is a T junction. Turn right and you will reach San Miguel in 4km (2½ miles). Turn left and the twisting, bumpy road will take through

Carnival time at Los Cristianos is a colourful celebration

Los Cristianos, once a small fishing village now caters for the tourist with its bustling pedestrianised shopping area

the arid land to the Los Abrigos/Las Chafiras junction on the *autopista*. **San Isidro** is well worth a visit and, like San Miguel, it provides many of the industrial requirements of the coastal resorts. It has a wide main street and parking is not a problem. There seems to be every possible shop here, spaced between the large car show-rooms and furniture warehouses, and a good selection of restaurants can be found here too. The road to Chimiche will lead you to the old southern road. Those with a sense of adventure should take the road leading west to La Parella. Found at the lower end of the town on a traffic light controlled junction, the road seems to be going nowhere. You are led alongside deserted *fincas*, protected in their fruitful days by the now weatherbeaten walls. Deserted houses exposed to the elements look forlornly out over the desert where only the cactus survives and in places even these have withered and died. You go under the au*topista* via a narrow bridge and emerge to view the contrasting lushness of the Golf del Sur with the continuing desert-like wilderness that leads down to the airport. At the T junction, turning right will bring you to the *autopista*, turn left and the fishing port of Los Abrigos is just beyond the low hills.

This region encompasses all the physical features of the south. The aridity of the area is easily visible and the land for which men fought hard to turn it into productive soil, only to abandon it again when tourism arrived. The south has industry, towns, villages and views of breathtaking splendour that contrast sea with mountain. It is so near to the resorts and yet so unexplored. These towns were here long before the tourists, and although they have changed and adapted, they retain a character that is as fascinating as it is tradi-tional.

The Costa del Silencio

Perhaps this 'Coast of Silence' was so named before the developers arrived or maybe it refers to the silence of the sea. Either way, this busy area makes full use of the romance of its name. The true boundaries are hard to define, although the area south of the autopista from the junction at Guaza to the El Medano interchange is included here. Although the Costa del Silencio is popular with tourists, the centre covers only a fraction of the coastline. There are still many villages that offer the appearance and atmosphere of a traditional port, but that is not to say they do not take note of the many visitors. Las Galletas has a superb marina where yachts berth alongside fishing vessels. Los Abrigos is a small village that has a reputation all over the island for having good fish restaurants. Almost everyone that comes to Tenerife visits the Costa del Silencio without realising it, for just inland is Reina Sofia Airport.

On leaving the *autopista* at Guaza, you immediately come to a crossroads. Turn right and you can take the old road back to Los Cristianos, although the surface is bad and best avoided. However, less than 1km (½ mile) up this road, while the surface is still acceptable, is the Desierto Feliz ('Happy Desert'). Here, for a small charge, excellent guides show you the plants and cacti of Tenerife. There is a small zoo that is well worth a visit.

Turn left at the crossroads and you run parallel to the *autopista* for 7km (4 miles) before reaching the Los Abrigos / San Miguel junction. The village of **Guaza** which you enter on leaving the *autopista*, seems a hotch potch of unfinished building where industry and restaurants thrive. Guaza is a small but important place offering support to the tourist business, and as you pass through you may note that the one road through is the 'only' road in town. After 2½ km (1½ miles) you meet another crossroads, after passing the Camel Safari. It seems strange to find these animals among the bananas, although the imposing peak of the Guaza mountain covered in scrub remind you that the desert 'home' of these beasts is to be found nearby. Recently a new golf course has been opened. A small 9 hole course, it is excellent for the new golfer and offers a pleasant and not undemanding change to those used to the big courses nearby.

Turning right at the crossroads will take you to **Palm Mar**. This village is a strange place. To one side building is going on, to the other it seems to have stopped and off the main road are a series of dust roads that divide some substantial and attractive villas. Palm Mar gives the impression that it could have a lot to offer if only it was finished, yet there often seems little evidence of continuing work. The beach is pleasant and if they ever go ahead and build the proposed tunnel between here and Los Cristianos it should become busy. Palm Mar has recently been the subject of a planned investment of many millions of pesetas and it should, in time, compete with its close and successful neighbours. Palm Mar is a dead end and you return to the crossroads.

Approaching the crossroads from Guaza, turning left will take you to a T junction, 3km (2 miles) just above the entrance to Ten Bel. A longer but more interesting route is to carry straight on towards the coast. If you follow the junction El Fraille is on the right and at first seems little more than another collection of unfinished breeze block dwellings. This village, like so many in the area, is developing as a direct result of its proximity to the main holiday centre. If the attractive church is an indication of the care the inhabitants are taking in the buildings then eventually El Fraille will become a modern but well cared for village. Many of the roads have yet to be finished but it is worth driving through towards the church and exploring the streets for the excellent selection of quality eating places to be found. The beach lies just past the village, as the road bears left into Las Galletas, look for the dirt entrance on the right. A car park of sorts is available and from here it is just a short walk to an enclosed beach with little areas of sand spread among the rocks. The sea is often calm and ideal for swimming.

Las Galletas is a mixture of the traditional and contemporary. The aforementioned harbour is a mixture of the two — a safe haven for the inshore fishing boats and a berth for expensive cruisers. The village itself lives in the shadow of Ten Bel and the other complexes. Las Galletas has a narrow rock and shingle beach, popular with the Canarians. It shelves steeply so is not ideal for bathing. Behind the wide walkway that runs parallel to the main street is a promenade where it is possible to enjoy a quiet evening walk, stopping occasionally in the bars, so near to the hurly burly of the resorts, yet far enough away to escape from them.

As you leave Las Galletas heading inland, the glass and concrete of **Ten Bel** appears. Just before the Shell station is the right hand turn that will take you into the heart of the resort. Shops, discos and apartment blocks form the centre of the Costa del Silencio. Although the area is popular with holidaymakers it is not unattractive, just busy.

If you want to avoid the township, carry straight on, and after 2km (1 mile) you can turn left to return to the crossroads above El Fraille. Carry straight on and within 1½km (1 mile) you enter the village of **Guargacho**. Guargacho can be approached from the south. By entering the main road at the Shell station, drive on through the resort until the right hand bend at the end of the straight. On the bend is the bust of the 'founder' of this eastern end, Alfonso Tavio. His family are still very much involved with the area and Amarilla Golf in particular. Follow the bend round and, as the road straightens, take the left hand turn. The more modern road continues ahead but at present leads nowhere. By taking the brief but bumpy track after the unfinished and abandoned apartment block, you join the tarmac road and after 2½km (1½ miles) this brings you to Guargacho. Look out to your left, and you will occasionally see patches of lush green grass, in sharp contrast to the barren desert at the roadside. Just over the hills are two splendid golf courses (see Fact File for further information), nursed from the desert and now offering excellent facilities for golfers and spectators alike.

Beyond Guargacho the road twists towards the *autopista*. After a few kilometres you join the road linking Guaza and Las Chafiras. This road frequently climbs and descends before the surface improves at this junction. Turn left and you return to Guaza in 5km (3 miles). This road provides excellent views across the low plain to the sea. In the foreground are the plantations of bananas, in the distance the white, hazy shapes of the costa. Turn right and pass the new but unequipped fire station, the warehouses and the entrance to Amarilla Golf and you reach Las Chafiras and the *autopista* after 2km (1 mile). Turning left at the junction gives you access to the motorway. By going left and then straight on, you reach San Miguel in the hills. This road is very important as one of the distribution centres for the beer Dorada is here. Many are convinced that this local brew is the life blood of the island and without it Tenerife would not be the same.

By turning left at Las Chafiras you enter the Saharan wilderness of the coast on the road to Los Abrigos. Here the barren, sand-coloured rock shimmers in the midday heat, so that you could be forgiven for thinking that the pastures of Golf Del Sur over the *barranco* are a mirage. The wind often howls through the valleys and fells, lifting sand from the rock to form a dust cloud. A little over 1km (½ mile) from the junction is a road that leads to San Isidro. As you negotiate the next 2km (1 mile) to Los Abrigos, you may well hear the whine of jet engines, for the airport lies over the hill to your left.

Los Abrigos is famous for its fish restaurants. At the T junction head straight on and the port lies around the bend. Here boats of all shapes and sizes compete for space with the local children as they show off their diving and swimming skills, leaping from the quay into the water below. This port has grown as its popularity has increased. Take time to walk through the narrow lanes behind the restaurants, where simple bars are available for refreshment, some seemingly little more than a converted front room. Around the headland that shelters the port are a number of small bays, where steps are thoughtfully provided for those wishing to swim in the azure sea.

By turning left at the junction, you bypass much of Los Abrigos. The road is in excellent condition and rises and falls like a rollercoaster towards El Medano. Along the 7km (4 miles) stretch are a number of entrances that lead to the sea. The beaches are large and

The rugged landscape above Arona with its sparse vegetation

Vilaflor, the highest parish in Tenerife, sits among some of the island's most beautiful scenery

'sandy', the shingle is very fine but shelter from the wind can be difficult to find. Along the way you will see the signs for 'Hermano Pedro'. This man is a saint-like figure to many Canarians and up the short track that heads towards the airport is a shrine in a cave where photos of those who seek his blessing are hung like tiles. It certainly makes for a different and unusual stopping place.

To the left is desert, broken only by wind-damaged greenhouses and *barrancos*. On the coastal side is Costa Bella. Well signposted, this new development awaits to be finished. The roads have been laid for nearly 2 years, strange tarmac veins running into the heart of the desert. The lamp-posts, like sentries, keep vigil over the quiet and deserted roads. Keep an eye out for a solitary building that looks like a control tower. Enter the concrete expanse and drive with the building on your right towards the sea. From the headland there is an excellent view of El Medano beach and, if the windsurfers are at sea, you can marvel at their skill as they race towards the coast, tacking at the last moment to speed out to sea again. The beach at El Medano can be reached from alongside the hotel.

The village of **El Medano** is reached by turning right at the T junction. The intersection illustrates the nautical influence in the locality, a traditional fishing boat stands guard. El Medano has established itself as a resort and port. Developers are busy at work next to a modern harbour where fishing boats moor at the end of the day. The narrow beach that is enclosed by the port is busy on Sundays and bank holidays, but you should find space to relax in mid-week, taking one of the many good walks, enjoying the sun and watching the fishermen at work. It can be windy but shelter is available on the beach.

From El Medano the road leads back to the *autopista* and the San Isidro junction to the east of the airport, 3½ km (2 miles) away. The coastal walk between the ports of El Medano and Los Abrigos is interesting and not too strenuous. Here the desert meets the sea and the wind whips up the water. A taxi or a bus will bring you back to the car.

Additional Information

Places of Interest

Desierto Feliz
Outside Los Cristianos on Guaza road. Cacti abound here in a desert-like complex. Talks and tours on the plants. Free bus.
Open: daily 10am-6pm.

Bananera Jardines del Atlantico
Between Guaza and Valle San Lorenzo
An interesting visit that allows you to discover all about the water system in Tenerife. As well as a museum, there are tropical plants etc. Open: daily 10am-6pm.

Chasna Artesian Centre
Craft workshop on the road from Arona to Vilaflor. Local handicrafts and wine are sold here.
Open: daily 10am-1pm and 4-7pm.

Playa de las Americas
Casino
Below Pueblo Canario
Passport essential.
Opens until late.
☎ 79 37 12

El Medano
Zoo. Los Cristianos.
Close to Deiserto feliz on the old road from Los Cristianos to Guaza. A small but well presented range of animals. Free bus from many locations.

Aguapark – Octopus Park
San Eugenio Alfo
Open: all year 10am-6pm
Free bus from many hotels.
☎ 79 22 66

Las Aguilas Del Teide
Nature reserve, shows, ecological park.
Signposted on the road from Los Cristianos to Arona
Open: 9am-7pm
☎ 72 50 61

Tourist Information Centres

Playa de las Americas
Parque Santiago
Open: Monday to Friday 9am-1pm and 4-7pm. Saturday 9am-1pm.
☎ 79 76 68

Las Galletas
El Muelle
Open: Monday to Friday 9am-1pm and 4-7pm. Saturday 9am-1pm.
☎ 73 01 33

El Medano
La Plaza
Open: Monday to Friday 9am-1pm and 4-7pm. Saturday 9am-1pm.
☎ 17 60 02

2
EASTERN TENERIFE

B efore the construction of the southern *autopista*, the journey from
   Los Cristianos to Santa Cruz was along the old inland road. No
matter how you view the *autopista*, you have to experience the old
route to understand how much of a blessing the motorway that runs
from the Fañabe to Santa Cruz is. The roads run almost parallel,
closing and parting along the way, joined by a number of small roads
that previously were used to transport the residents of the hills down
to the coast. The two roads could not be more different. The *autopista*
carves its way along the coast with little concession to the terrain or
gradient. The inland route twists and turns over *barrancos* and
through sleepy villages that before the construction of the *autopista*
must have shaken and resounded to the noise of lorries, coaches and
cars. Today it is as quiet as it is spectacular. Both roads will be looked
at in turn.

The Autopista

Most people use the *autopista* as a fast route between two points,
more often than not the resorts of Las Americas and Los Cristianos
and Santa Cruz. Along its route and just beyond the frequent
junctions are many places worth visiting. El Medano and San Isidro
lie just off Junction 21 and Junction 20 is 3½km (2 miles) east. From
here you can climb to Chimiche but, as you come off the motorway
and climb onto the bridge, look out for the rough track that leads
towards the coast. There is no sign to indicate that anything lies
down the dusty but passable track but the lane leads through the
desert to an oasis near the coast.

Within 1km (½ mile) you will have spotted the village lying
beyond the *fincas* of tomatoes. **Las Maretas del Rio** is a strange and

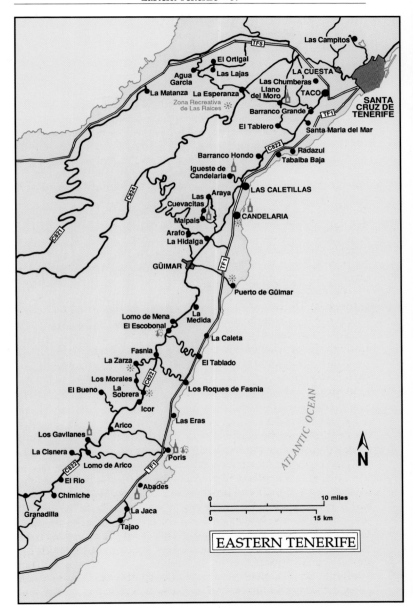

EASTERN TENERIFE

haunting place but a delightful village nevertheless. Across the desert, roads etched in the rock and dust lead to the sea. The large, half finished houses are proof that the area is not poor, just out of the way. Follow the road to the sea and pass the little plaza with a church that must be one of the smallest on the island. There is a compact beach that is ideal for swimming and it is possible to fish from the beach or rocks. The village has a character that is not apparent at first, it may have developed in recent years but one is left to wonder how it came to exist at all. Visit the small bar, sponsored by the Asociación de Vecinos, a neighbourhood group. There you can have a quiet drink in the company of the locals, a friendly crowd who will make you welcome. Find time to walk along the coast where the desert is contoured in strange and fascinating shapes. There are ample places to have a quick swim to get rid of the dust.

The next junction on the autopista (number 19) also offers a place to swim and fish, or take refreshment. Coming off the *autopista*, follow the signs to **Tajao**. Fishing seems to be the main industry in the village, and locals gather in the plaza under the shadow of the church to tell of the day's catch and 'the one that got away'. At the far end of the village take the track to the right and follow the road. Just past the modern block of buildings is a small beach that offers excellent swimming. If you continue onwards the coastline, shaped by the wind, offers a number of small, sandy inlets. By the junction is the road to La Jaca. The narrow road is little more than a tarmac strip laid across the rocks. After 1½km (1 mile) there is a track off to the right, the rustic signpost points to **La Jaca**. The road drops into the remote, tranquil village and parking is conveniently positioned outside the bar. The beach is small and there is a small harbour where the fishing boats sway at anchor. There are natural swimming pools and steps lead from the play area into the sea.

Follow the road beyond the turning to La Jaca and through the barren infertile desert and you drive parallel to the *autopista*. At times the fast flowing traffic is next to the track, separated only by a loose pile of rocks. After 3½km (2 miles) you reach Junction 18. Rather than rejoin the *autopista*, turn left towards the sea and down the short road to **Abades**. This village has a superb beach that is rarely crowded. It is small, sandy, quiet and well-positioned. The area is beginning to see development, neat bungalows with grass front gardens have been built in neat rows off the main road. As you head towards the sea, there are two churches. The more recent one is small but attractive, while behind it, on the hill, is a large, seemingly ruined church. It was here in the last centuries that the leper colony was sited, and those who suffered from other diseases were brought here. Where the bungalows start the road surface improves and it continues to the sea. Even on Sundays, when it can be crowded, there is plenty of room and in the week it is deserted, waiting to be discovered.

The tourist industry has in the main left the areas east of El Medano alone. For that reason **Poris** is something of a mystery. Leave the *autopista* at Junction 17 and before you lie neat villas and beyond them large aparthotels. Building continues as the area certainly seems popular with the Canarians, and the town supports a greater number of residents than visitors. There is a wide choice of excellent restaurants, shops, banks and, of course, there is the sea. Take the road towards the sea and follow the road to the right, keep on the road and when you see the Casa Julian restaurant turn left. Turn right by the phone box and opposite the playground take the road on the right. This road will take you past beaches that are sheltered and inviting. The road gets a little rough in places but is passable. Within 1km (½ mile) you pass evidence of a proposed but now deserted development, the rusting lamposts and kerbstones standing weathered and silent. The road leads into a large plaza. On the headland at **Punta Abona** is a lighthouse with spectacular views, while from the ground you can look back on Poris and westwards along the craggy coast. The church is charming but so large that you are left to wonder where the congregation lives, for there are only a few houses here. There is a bar and a small, friendly restaurant. Poris is as strange as it is undiscovered. With the demand for quiet coastal resorts and accommodation increasing, those in the know will see Poris as an attractive and convenient alternative.

Las Eras, reached by leaving the autopista at Junction 16, is a friendly village. It seems to be waiting to be finished, but this does not detract from its character. It has a church no bigger than a garage and a small beach where you can paddle or swim in the low surf or explore the rock pools. There is also a restaurant.

Junction 15 is only available for those who wish to change direction. Junction 14 leads either north or south. Heading north takes you to Fasñia (pronounced Fan nya). The town is 6km (4 miles) away, on the old southern road and is described in more detail in 'The Old Road East section'. The rocks on the coast take their name from Fasñia, from where the villagers descend to the sea on restdays. The Roques de Fasñia are two large islands of lava. One has been reclaimed, stands to the rear of the village and houses the church. To the right of the bar is a small track that will lead to a car park from

Punta Abona's simple church seems to overwhelm the village

Punta Abona's quiet beach

where the rocks can be viewed. By turning left before the village the track will lead to a pebble beach that is popular with sun lovers and swimmers alike.

Although the natural inclination is to look towards the coast, do not forget to glance inland from time to time; Teide and its foothills are there to be seen and admired. The land is more fertile inland, a tribute to the endeavour of the farming communities in the hills. The green is splashed with the white buildings of the villages and farms. Tanks filled with precious water glint in the sun, evidence that here at least tourism has not replaced agriculture as the main employer. The inhabitants seem divided by the *autopista*, which runs close to the sea here. Those to the inland side are farmers, while those nearer the sea are fishermen. Although their sons and daughters may have been attracted by nearby Santa Cruz, it must be hard for them to sever all ties with the peace and tranquillity these places offer.

The hamlets between Junctions 13 and 14 are as typically Canarian as you will find on the coast. At Junction 13 you can head up to Escobanal which, like Fasñia, is on the old road and there is more information about it in the following section. To the seaward side is **El Tablado** which has a small rocky beach. As you leave the junction turn left, not over the bridge but alongside it, and follow the road down by the sea and along the shore. Where the lava meets the sea is a shoreline of infinite variety and considerable beauty. The road climbs and descends, following the easiest route through the rock. **Punta Prieta** has been built around a hole in the rock, a cave-like structure that houses the fishermens' boats, nets, pots and lines. In the bay is a natural harbour that has seen little change for decades.

The road emerges at Junction 12. Before rejoining the *autopista*, head towards **La Caleta**, the turning is signposted on the right. Apart from a small pebble beach there seems little here until you spy the natural swimming pool behind the houses, here you can join the locals in a seawater pool that is cleaned by the swell and tide.

Emerging from La Caleta, turn right and the road, which is a dead end, will lead to **El Espignon**. Here the rocks emerge from the sea and form rock pools where you can explore and try your hand at catching the small fish unlucky enough to be trapped in the ebbing tide. The villages all have bars and, as always, you will be made welcome.

Our journey along the southern *autopista* will, for the moment, end at **Puerto de Güimar**. This area is being developed but the change appears gradual and is in keeping with the character of the port. The town square is dominated by a memorial.

The beach here has been extended along the coast and groynes have been built to break the power of the tide. There is ample car parking close to the Club Nautico which is approached by turning right just before the square.

Around the square are a number of restaurants and bars — there is even a fast food burger/pizza café, a rare sight out of the resorts. The beach is large and usually quiet. Beyond the shallows and the sea wall, windsurfers are often to be seen, racing across the bay. To the west is a private and seemingly exclusive yacht club (entry on foot is permitted). There is ample parking along the promenade and even if it is only to break your journey briefly, Puerto de Güimar will always provide something of interest to see and do. The port takes its name from Güimar which is the large town visible from the *autopista*, nestling in the valley.

At Junction 11, turn inland and the road climbs quickly to enter the town which is 5km (3 miles away). Güimar is on the old road east and is described in more detail in the following section. It is one of the most important agricultural towns on the island and is is also a crossroads which makes it a logical place to end the section of the book devoted to the southern coast. From here there is easy access to the *autopista*, the National Park and the north of the island. The importance of the junction has perhaps been lessened by the building of the motorway, but the town is a busy, bustling place and there is always something of interest to note. The old south route splits at Güimar. It starts in Los Cristianos to which we now return to follow the route east.

The Old Road East

As you climb away from the coast, at La Camella, turn left for Arona and Teide. By carrying straight on you travel through to Granadilla. It is here the old southern road really starts.

As you travel this road, it is interesting to note that until the southern *autopista* was built in the 1970s, this was the main road between Santa Cruz and the developing south. It is hard to imagine the chaos that would have ensued had the development gone ahead without the relief of the motorway. The inland road is narrow, twisting and not always in good repair. The scenery varies; it can be green one moment, barren the next, and villages are passed quickly, reflecting the declining importance of this road in recent years. However, it is this that gives it character and makes the trip worthwhile. In places it seems you are in a time warp where faded signs advertise bars that are no longer open and where drinks are no longer sold as the customers now travel at speed along the *autopista* below.

Granadilla is an important junction. One can travel north through Vilaflor and on to the National Park, south to San Isidro, east to Güimar. The town centre is large and well served with shops and banks and is in many ways the 'capital' of the south. The Property and Land Registry and courts are here, as well as a number of important offices. Granadilla has a history that can be traced way back before the tourist boom. As an important market town, it has always been a focal point for many of the nearby towns and villages and it remains so today.

Within a few hundred yards of leaving Granadilla and following the signs for Güimar, the character of the journey is set. A variety of scenery, colour and beauty changes at every bend and junction. Although there is a junction after 5½km (3½ miles) that will take you down through the desert to San Isidro, it is worth persevering. You will quickly realise that the roadbuilders were forced to submit to the contours of the land while, as the crow flies, the distance between villages is often very little. The road twists and turns along the side of the *barrancos*, crossing at the most convenient point where the valley is narrow and shallow.

The bridges are narrow and stonebuilt and often there is room for only one car. However, the road is quiet and you will rarely meet oncoming traffic. Taking your time is important here as the surface, condition and route of the road mean that it is not one to be taken in a hurry. That is just as well because at speed you would miss a great deal. The villages through which you pass rely on agriculture as the main source of income. You will see *fincas* (plots of land) and the sand-coloured walls, hewn and built by hand which retain the soil and provide protection from the eroding effects of the wind.

Shortly after the junction to San Isidro is the village of **Chimiche**, followed a few kilometres later by **El Rio. La Cisnera** comes and goes almost without being noticed, a small collection of tidy houses that spread inland and up the hill. **Lomo de Arico** is an important local town for several reasons, particularly as it has a cinema. As a junction it allows a return to the coast at Poris, 8km (5 miles) away. Turning inland and following the signs to Valle de Contador will take you above the town. This provides an opportunity to look back and down across the cultivated land and into the *barrancos* (there is also an excellent barbecue area here).

The road continues onto Los Gavilanes. Perhaps the steeple of the church here was added as an afterthought for it stands apart from the

The old road east passes through a mainly undeveloped, natural landscape

Granadilla is an important market town where the church acts as a focus for the surrounding community

main body of the building. Arico Nuevo (New) and Arico Viejo (Old) are situated either side of another road that leads for 5km (3 miles) down to Poris. These busy villages stand astride a *barranco* where the industrious farmers have claimed as much land as possible. Terracing the side of the *barranco* has altered the character of these dry rivers but added colour to the arid features of the valley. You will find somewhere to eat and drink in all the villages, even if it is just a small local bar. In Arico, not all the restaurants that served the road in its heyday have closed and, although their menus will be limited, the food is as good and traditional as the welcome you will receive.

The following kilometres reflect the ghostly character this road sometimes displays. In the heat of the afternoon as the ground shimmers distorting the view, you may find the streets of **Icor** deserted. The workers are early risers, some will have been in the fields at 5.30am, working before the sun climbs from behind the high hills to the east. In the afternoon they take a well-earned siesta, dozing behind the rustic wooden windows oblivious to your passing. While the workers rest, some of the older women talk, as they sit in their doorways and watch the world go slowly by. They will nod in response to your wave, their sun-stained faces barely acknowledging your presence. Many of the older village folk will have lived and worked within a few kilometres all their lives; occasionally visiting Santa Cruz, Güimar and, in their younger days, walking or riding by donkey or mule to the coast.

In Icor is a junction that leads to **El Bueno**, 3km (2 miles) up in the hills. It is a small and charming village, worth a quick visit if only to explore off the main road and enjoy the views offered in every direction. **Los Morales** is a matter of minutes from Icor. Approached from the east, it seems to be little more than two houses either side of the *barranco*, but approached from Granadilla the village is seen spread out, basking in the sun. Dirt tracks lead to the neat, traditional houses and dwellings.

One and a half kilometres (1 mile) beyond the sign that announces Los Morales (coming in from Icor) is a road that is easy to miss. The track climbs quickly as you pass through neat *fincas*, providing crops to support the villages of **La Sobrera** and **La Zarza**. These tiny rustic villages are traditional, beautiful and untouched by the outside world. There are bars in the two villages and try to find time to enjoy the views and take in the very special atmosphere these hamlets possess. Climb for 6km (4 miles) and then return down to the main road at Fasnia. By carrying straight on at Los Morales, along the primary route, you will continue into Fasñia.

Fasñia offers another chance to return to the coast which is 6km (4 miles) away. There is a small church in the plaza just below the main road, and Fasñia also has a number of bars and restaurants. It is an important place for local agriculture and is surrounded by some delightful villages. Beyond the town the road to El Escobonal leads through the sand-coloured land. The *fincas* often lack soil here so the crops are grown in pumice taken from the hills and valleys around Teide. Potatoes, vines and flowers are all grown on the terraces that cling to the side of the *barrancos*. Every available piece of land has been used, so that where the gradient is steep, terraces have been built.

During your travels around Tenerife, you will often see narrow water canals. In many prosperous areas, and on the large collectives, canals have been replaced with pipes. However, here, as in many parts of the island, open handmade canals, often many decades old, are still used to supply the fields with water. The system can be very intricate, and like a railway they have point systems to divert water from one *finca* to another. All are gravity fed from large tanks, which in turn are supplied from the hills above the towns and villages. As the road twists and rolls between Fasnia and El Escobonal and beyond, the scene is one of man's management of the land against the odds. Beyond El Escobonal keep an eye open for the aqueduct. The obvious effort put into building this structure illustrates the lengths to which the locals will go in making the most of the seemingly inhospitable and unworkable land.

At El Escobonal there is yet another chance to rejoin the motorway. The trip down to the coast and the main road reveals the change in terrain as you get closer to the sea. By the time you reach the coast the sand-coloured rock has changed to the black lava and the beaches have little areas of black 'sand' between the rock pools. The wind is an important factor here for, as it whips in from the sea, it erodes the top soil to reveal the hardy base stone below. Walls built to prevent this are found in most areas of Tenerife; occasionally in bad repair, their crumbling walls witness to the deserted *fincas* and the move towards tourism as a source of income.

Continuing towards Güimar on the inland road, beyond the junction, is **El Escobonal** itself. Perhaps its proximity to the junction has helped it to retain some of the bars that other villages have lost with the decline in the road's importance. A few kilometres later you pass through Lomo de Mena and then La Medida, two small bustling villages that have retained their rustic charm.

Two kilometres (1 mile) after La Medida, on a bend, is the strange sight of a large and seemingly well-fitted hotel. It seems so out of place, perched high above Güimar, but look closer and you notice the 'Closed' sign. This building, perhaps more than any other on the route, illustrates the decline in business along this road. The painted walls are faded, the pool is empty and the bars and terraces are silent. Stop here using the deserted car park, and walk about 100m (110yd) to the *mirador*. This is perhaps one of the most spectacular viewpoints in Tenerife and yet you will find few cameras pointing into the valley below. The uninterrupted view is of Güimar and the *fincas* that surround the town. Beyond the town the hills rise to meet the sky. From here it is difficult to appreciate the activity below.

Only when you travel to the valley floor does it become apparent that this sunken plain boasts fertile land and is a hive of agricultural activity. If you have chosen a clear day for your visit, look seawards and you may catch the outline of Gran Canaria on the horizon. To the right, the terraces on the valley sides are close enough to pick out the individual crops. Very little of the available space has been left to nature, for the terraces are in view everywhere. It really is a superb viewpoint and one that should not be missed. From the *mirador* the road drops to the valley floor and into Güimar.

Güimar has been an important site throughout the history of Tenerife. The Mencey (Guanche Prince) Añaterve had not joined the main force against the Spanish. He had opted to fight alone but in the end became a faithful ally of the invaders. Today Güimar is a large although somewhat disparate town. It is an important agricultural centre and market town with a variety of shops in a centre of interesting architecture and traditional character. From here you can head north through Arafo to connect with the La Laguna/Teide road. Carry straight on, and the road continues, eventually coming into Santa Cruz. Heading south will take you directly down to Junction 11 of the *autopista* and Puerto de Güimar. This is a small but growing leisure and residential complex that can satisfy the needs of the traveller and explorer alike. It is described in more detail earlier, in the Autopista section.

Stay on the *autopista*, and Junction 10 leads to Arafo. The junction is confusing when approached from the west, as you must take the second of the two slip roads. The route swings under the motorway and climbs away from the coast. After about 3km (2 miles) you meet a T junction which is an extension of the old inland route. This route goes all the way to Santa Cruz and will be explored in greater detail later.

Junction 9 is the entrance to **Candelaria**. This is one of the most

This view of Güimar shows the importance of agriculture in the area

The church at Güimar is built in a local style

The Basilica de Candelaria dominates the town and is well worth a visit for its magnificent interior

important towns on the island, not because of industry, agriculture and the beach, but for the Basilica de Candelaria which houses the ✳ statue of the 'Virgen' which all islanders know as 'Nuestra Senora de Candelaria' (Our lady of Candelaria). This statue is subject of legend; it is believed that the statue was washed up on shore and discovered by fishermen. The lady appeared to the Guanches long before the Spanish arrived and they worshipped the image. When the conquest was over the Spanish built a small church to house the statue. The virgin and the church were destroyed in the nineteenth century, but today there is a second statue in the splendid basilica, built in the colonial style of the islands, which rises above the town and can be seen from the *autopista*.

The simple exterior of the basilica contrasts with the magnificence of the interior and particularly the virgin herself. Rather than being hidden away, like so many treasures, she stands on top of her platform — draped in gold and silk cloth, adorned with gold and jewels, her serene face innocent and the baby Jesus in her arms. Throughout the year flowers are placed at her feet and those wishing her favours kneel, touch the ribbon that flows from her clothes and make their wish. The basilica is a place of worship and although visitors are welcomed, their attention is drawn to signs regarding behaviour and dress. You are not allowed entry if you are wearing bathing suits, untidy clothes, shorts or 'revealing' dress. For those of the Catholic faith there are regular services to which you will be welcome, and candles can be lit in a small area to the side of the nave.

The church stands at the side of an open plaza guarded by the stone statues of the Guanches Kings. The sea laps at the beach just behind these impressive sentinels. There are plenty of bars and fish restaurants along the roads leading to the church, together with a number of souvenir shops.

On Sundays and holidays the road system around the town is closed, allowing pedestrian traffic to walk to the plaza. In any case, as you leave the *autopista* and head down into Candelaria, it is far easier to park and walk, enjoying the very special atmosphere the town offers. Should you wish to swim, there is a small beach behind the main street which, although narrow and at times battered by the surf, provides a place for a cooling dip. However, swimming is not advisable at high tide or in rough weather. Depending on the day of your visit, you may find a market and funfair in the car park to the left of the start of the one way system.

If Santa Cruz is not your destination and you want to head north to the coast or back along the south coast, then the junction at Candelaria can provide access to the island's interior. By turning off at the Candelaria junction and heading inland, you come to a T junction. This road arrives from the west, having started above Los Cristianos. After Guimar it continues for 4km (2½ miles) to La Hidalga, above Junction 10. There are two routes from here that will take you to above Junction 9 on the *autopista*. The most direct way is to follow the road from La Hidalga without turning off. This route will take you through the rich agricultural area above Candelaria.

A more interesting and more complex network of roads is to be found by turning left just after leaving La Hidalga and following the signs to Araya, ½km (¼ mile) from the T junction. Between the two junctions is a pattern of routes, all of which interconnect and are of interest. Having turned left at the junction you pass the Arafo Donkey Safari, and soon after is a turning on the left signposted **Malpais**. The name means 'bad country', though the area is anything but this to the eye, for as you climb above the road the terraces are in use and well-tended.

The village of Malpais is spread out but you find yourself driving through a small village centre. Turn left before the church and the road continues over the undulating terrain for the short distance to **Las Cuevacitas**. This is a somewhat larger village that spreads from the road up into the hills, and keeping the unusual church on your left, follow the main track down until you rejoin the 'main' road. Turn left and the road leads into the village of Araya. At the T junction turn right and, after about 2km (1 mile), you reach the road just above the *autopista*. Junction 9 is a few hundred yards away, reached by turning left.

If you take this route in reverse by entering the area from above Candelaria, it is easy to miss the junctions, as the signposts are often only visible when it is too late to make the turn. These small communities are worth exploring and the views from their position above the coast are as different as they are interesting. Coming up from the *autopista* at Junction 9 will lead to the T junction previously noted, while turning right takes the route towards Santa Cruz, using the same old southern road.

Leaving Candelaria, the road twists through and across the *barrancos* where modern villas contrast sharply with the older traditional properties. Avocado and papaya grow in abundance here. After 2km (1 mile) the village of **Igueste de Candelaria** is signposted. The village clings to the slopes of the hills, a small collection of dwellings with a church that can be viewed from the road below. Beyond Igueste the road continues to be a succession of sharp bends and curves as it begins to climb. The view of the coast widens as the climb steepens — the Bay of Arenitas and Radazul can be seen below, and Gran Canaria appears as a dull ghost on the horizon.

After Junction 7 on the *autopista*, **Barranco Hondo** shows in the hills above the road, set in a countryside that can be seen to its full advantage as the road climbs steeply to skirt the mountain. The land spreads forth below, the abandoned terraces easily identified by the crumbling walls, an arid patchwork pattern on a green cloth. Radazul lies below, as does the power station at Las Caletillas, the smoke from the stacks drifting across an otherwise perfect view.

Tabaiba is about 3km (2 miles) after Barranco Hondo and provides a centre for the surrounding villages. The evidence of industry increases and continues now into Santa Cruz, but the occasional *finca* remains to provide a splash of colour.

Tabaiba is really the last country town before the capital, so if Santa Cruz is not your destination, it is better to turn up into the hills just after Tabaiba, where the road is clearly marked El Tablero TF4119. If you continue along the old road, you enter Santa Maria del Mar and Barranco Grande. Faced with such romantic names as these, you may be disappointed to find modern flats built next to large factories and warehouses. The road continues to Taco and joins the northern *autopista*.

The road to El Tablero quickly leaves industry behind and only the open cast mine remains, in contrast to the *fincas* and houses. The village of El Tablero, 1½km (1 mile) away, seems little more than a collection of roadside houses backed by *fincas*.

After the village there is a crossroads. Heading straight on is not recommended as the tarmac soon becomes dirt and the track narrows to loop across the hills to Llano del Moro. Turn right at the junction and the road arrives in Llano along a far better surface. There is much to see, including a spectacular man-made quarry just outside El Tablero. Its sheer sides are a thousand shades of red and only the lorries and cranes spoil this seemingly natural creation. The evidence of better days is to be noted in the rusting and decaying remains of the aggregate silos before the entrance to **Llano del Moro**. You emerge just south of the main town square, dominated by the church, where a right turn will lead back to Barranco Grande, turn left and the crossroads offers the choice of La Laguna to the right, the road leads to the old airport and joins the northern *autopista*, or La Esperanza, straight on. The left hand turning is where the aforementioned country track leads from El Tablero.

In El Tablero turn left at the crossroads and keep to the 'main track'. On leaving the village, you emerge in open country, the surface is bumpy but quite passable. After 1km (½ mile) you approach an unmarked junction. Turn right and climb the steep hill, and after 500m (550yd) follow the track around to the right, continuing up at the 'junction'. The views soon open out across the flat foothills, and the Anaga mountains are to be seen in the distance. The *fincas* are divided by the traditional rock walls so widespread in the region and as a means of taming the sometimes harsh, infertile environment.

Then abruptly the landscape becomes very lush, flowers grow in the shade of the water tank, bushes and shrubs burst into colour at the roadside and the occasional fig tree can be seen among the vines. ❋ The scar across the hill is a water canal, painstakingly designed constructed and maintained to bring the vital water to the *fincas* below. Beyond the small unnamed village is a track into the forest, 7km (4½ miles) away. The tarmac trail takes you into the heart of the forest and to the Zona Recreativa de Las Raices. It is here that the Generals, under Franco, put the final touches to the plans that led Spain into civil war. A memorial to El Caudillo (Franco) can be found among the pines, a tall stone obelisk surrounded and partly hidden by the erect trees.

The road from El Tablero joins the La Laguna — Teide road after 8km (5 miles). To the left lies the beautiful route to Portillo and the National Park. Turn right and you soon enter the delightful town of **La Esperanza** (which means The Hope). The town lies below the main road on the route to Llano del Moro. There are so many restaurants along the main route that if you intend to stop here for refreshment you will be spoilt for choice. Almost without exception, the restaurants in the town and beyond on the road to La Laguna offer excellent fare, cooked and presented to a high standard and at very reasonable cost. The wine from the area is excellent and offered in earthenware pitchers. There is a knack to pouring from these and wine has often been spilt by unwary travellers.

From La Esperanza the road continues through the tree-lined way, across the meadows and grasslands to the side of Los Rodeos airport and Junction 6 on the *autopista*. Take your time and head towards Tacoronte. The change from south to north is completed as you leave La Esperanza and take the turning 2km (1 mile) from the village's centre signposted for Tacoronte. The road climbs away from the town, only to descend again through the green fields and rolling hills. The land is actively cultivated; potatoes, vines and all manner of root crops are grown in the rich, brown soil. As the route passes the radio station and curves towards the coast the views open up to the northern *autopista* below. In the winter, almond trees in blossom sparkle in the sun, and houses nestle amongst the greenery.

Eight kilometres (5 miles) from La Esperanza you enter the busy crossroads town of Agua Garcia. Turning left here takes you towards Orotava. By turning right you pass quickly through the village of **Las Lajas**. At lunchtime the city workers gather here for their business lunches, while the villagers sit in their doorways and watch the visitors pass by.

El Ortigal is a larger village which lies close to the northern *autopista*, about 6km (4 miles) from Agua Garcia. The airport of Los Rodeos can be seen across the flat plain, beyond is the Anaga range and behind you Teide has risen into view. The junction with the northern *autopista* is reached 2km (1 mile) beyond El Ortigal. Turn left, towards Puerto de la Cruz; along the tree-lined avenue are some splendid houses, convenient for commuting into the capital a few kilometres away. The *autopista* runs parallel to this road. There are two junctions, the first allowing access to the eastbound carriageway for Santa Cruz. Soon after, at the entrance to the golf club (see Fact File for further information), the road swings under the main road and allows access to the western carriageway, Tacoronte and La Laguna. We shall return to the south here, taking the roads around the capital and into the Anaga. Eventually all the roads will lead to this junction on the *autopista*.

While the industry of the capital is very much in evidence now, there is still much of interest as the *autopista* nears the capital. Junction 8 allows access to the inland road at Igueste and down to the coast around the power station at Las Caletillas. Two kilometres (1 mile) later, Junction 7 allows an excursion to the same inland road at Barranco Hondo. Junction 6 again allows you to climb away from the coast to join the inland route at Tabaiba. You can also turn towards the coast and descend sharply to the quiet resort of **Tabaiba Baja**. This new resort is still growing and is hemmed in by the craggy rocks of the coast. Much thought has gone into the architecture and by following the road down, you travel through apartments, villas and bungalows to the sea. There is a small beach and a number of rocks from which you can dive. A quiet place, Tabaiba has yet to fulfill its potential. The bars and few restaurants offer a friendly atmosphere, far from the madding crowds.

When seen from above, **Radazul** (Junction 5) appears to be a sporting paradise. Tennis courts, pools and the marina suggest that this resort has much to offer. However, as you travel down you note that building is still going on and the resort seems to be waiting to open. There are boats in the marina, and those who own the villas are enjoying life in this tranquil resort. For the visitor there is much to see but surprisingly little to do, at least for the moment.

Junction 3 will take you up through the blocks of apartments that are Santa Maria del Mar to the inland road and access to the routes bypassing the capital. If you intend to bypass Santa Cruz and head west on the northern *autopista* then leave the motorway at Junction 2. It is well signposted Autopista Norte. Follow the road around and over the *autopista*, continue past the market entrance, and up past the cemetery. The road goes over the northern road and at the junction follow the road around to the right. At the traffic lights turn right and the road slips onto the northern *autopista* below Taco.

There is an extensive building programme of motorway construction being undertaken in Tenerife and the project will last for many years. Already the new northern and southern junctions are being prepared at Santa Maria del Mar and close to the existing junction as Somosierra. In addition plans are being prepared to replace the existing northern motorway as it nears La Laguna with a new road that will travel behind the airport at Los Rodeos. It is impossible to say how long these projects will take. Signposts will indicate the new routes and the diversions that will no doubt be in place whilst work goes on. It is worth noting that the road markings are usually in yellow where road works are being carried out. Caution is a good idea where these markings are present.

Santa Cruz de Tenerife

Just after Junction 2 the southern *autopista* splits. The left hand lane is signed for Las Ramblas, the right for Avenida Maritima. Your decision will be based on why you are visiting the capital. If you want to avoid driving in the city there is a simple route to a car park that is near the main shopping centre and many of the sights and historic buildings of the capital. As the *autopista* splits, stay in the right hand lane for Avenida Maritima. The road drops away to join the incoming northern road and forms a four lane road heading straight towards the port — get in the lane second in from the right at the last set of traffic lights. It can be very confusing as the left filter light is over a lane where you can only go straight on. In the sun it is not always possible to see the arrow shape and many drivers will stop. Follow it down and, at the last set of lights, follow the traffic flow around to the left. You are now running parallel to the port. The car park entrance is not easy to find. There is a large advertising hoarding just past the entrance and if you use that as a marker and slow down, you should not miss the entrance. After you have found a space, walk across the road into the Plaza de España and Santa Cruz opens before you. It is worth noting that the car park is staffed and your car is guarded. A tip of 100 ptas is considered ample for the guards.

Santa Cruz is a modern city where nearly one third of the population of Tenerife live. Like any large metropolis it has good and bad points, but the latter are quickly forgotten as you explore and

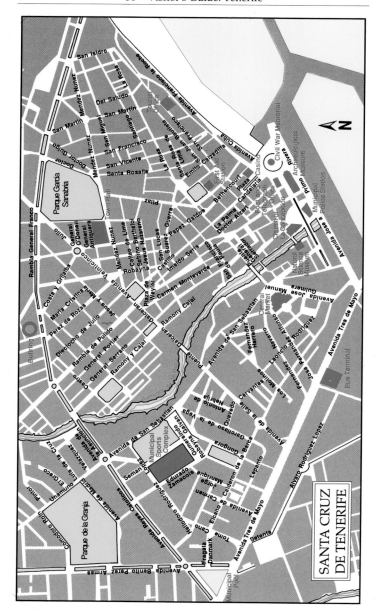

Relax from all the sight-seeing in one of Santa Cruz's pleasant parks

Santa Cruz, the capital of Tenerife, has much to offer the visitor

discover the character of a capital that is so different from the rest of Tenerife and from the sprawling capitals of Europe.

The site of today's capital dates from the fourteenth century when the arriving Spanish, who landed nearby, developed the site. Many of today's thoroughfares existed by the sixteenth century. The Spanish strength as a maritime nation contributed to the development of Santa Cruz, and the port is one of the deepest natural harbours in the world. This maritime influence is also evident in Lanzarote, where the Spanish moved the capital from inland Tegueste to today's coastal site at Arrecife. Only one of the capitals in the Canary Islands remains inland, Valverde on El Hierro. Using Tenerife as a stop for replenishing the stores on their galleons that went to the New World, the Spanish made Santa Cruz a fortress. Fear of attack from the English and pirates saw forts and gun emplacements being positioned around the port.

Today ships from all around the world arrive to unload and load their cargoes. Atlantic trawlers use the port for shelter and resupplying, and the port is a popular stopping-off point for the navies of the world. Tenerife relies heavily on imports and from the dockside you can watch container ships unloading next to the through-deck car transporters from which a seemingly endless flow of new cars emerges for the hire fleets of the island.

Santa Cruz is not only the capital of Tenerife but also the administrative capital of the province of islands that includes Tenerife, Gomera, El Hierro and La Palma. Accordingly, there are a number of government buildings including the parliament which meets here and also in Las Palmas de Gran Canaria. The military also maintain a large presence in the capital with a number of barracks including the general headquarters of the Canary Islands. As one would expect, many of the islands commercial companies have their head offices in Santa Cruz as do the government organisations such as the telephone company, social security and others. It is an unfortunate fact that many residents of Tenerife look upon Santa Cruz as a bureaucratic jungle to be avoided at all costs. This is a great shame as, behind the façade of modern offices, lies a city of charming character and one that has something of interest for everyone.

The Plaza de España is a familiar landmark to all who visit Santa Cruz and is a convenient place to start a tour of the city. The memorial that dominates the plaza honours the dead of Tenerife who fell in the Civil War. Around the obelisk are attractive gardens and the carnival is centred around the plaza. Alongside the plaza are a number of official buildings, the Cabildo Insular is the 'Home Office', and here also is the main post office and the excellent Museo Arqueologico (Archaeological Museum). This museum is well worth a visit, inside there are informative displays of Guanche artifacts and all manner of displays relating to the history of Tenerife.

Opposite the plaza is the modern shopping centre, around the Plaza Candelaria. The marble statue dates from 1778. This is one of the oldest roads in the capital, although now closed to traffic. The area is a busy commercial centre of shops and cafés, offices and hotels. If you are in the capital for a shopping trip, it is as well to take your time and wander further into the heart of the city. While the Plaza Candelaria and the adjoining streets are the principal centre, there are a number of shops further up the hill and these continue up to the Ramblas. In the Cabildo Insular building is the Tourist Office, where a number of free maps of the capital are available and the guide will be happy to advise you should you have a particular interest. You can also wander through the tree-lined avenues, experiencing the atmosphere.

Some of the most attractive features of Santa Cruz are the frequent parks and plazas. Some are no more than small squares set among the buildings and shielded from the heat of the day by the highrise sides of offices and shops. Others, like the Plaza de Weyler, are large open expanses of flower beds and walks with bars and cafés where you can rest your feet and quench your thirst. It is worth noting that the British Consulate is housed in Plaza de Weyler, appropriately above Barclays Bank.

By following the pedestrian way out of the top of Plaza de Candelaria you arrive in the Plaza de Weyler. The military headquarters are across the plaza. The municipal park can be reached by following the road that passes across the top of the plaza. Leave the plaza by the north-west exit and follow the road (Avenida de 25 de Julio). This road leads to the Ramblas and the park (Parque Garcia Sanabria) adjoins the junction of the two thoroughfares. As you stroll through the tree-lined walks, shaded from the sun, the busier parts of the capital are forgotten, and birdsong is heard instead of the roar of traffic. The park is a popular spot for the office workers to take their lunch, a sanctuary away from the pressures of work. Having a 3 hour lunch break gives them time to return home to the suburbs but many remain to amble through the park before taking lunch in one of the many nearby bars.

Although Santa Cruz is not the capital of the Catholic Church in Tenerife, the city does have a number of interesting churches. The parish church of La Concepcion is situated at the junction of Calle

The Plaza de España is a convenient starting point for tours of Santa Cruz

A fountain in the attractive Plaza de Weyler, Santa Cruz

Candelaria and Calle Calzada. This was built in 1502 and was recently restored. A number of relics and articles of historic significance are kept here; one of the flags captured from Nelson is displayed, as is part of the Cross. There are many churches of interest in the capital, and at many street corners you will find churches and chapels open to the public.

The city is divided by a *barranco*. Water flows down in a narrow stream, and grass grows on the marshy sides. It is sad that the view is spoiled by tipping rubbish and waste into the ravine. The Mercado de Nuestra Señora de Africa is a large and bustling market where some of the best bargains are to be found. The market lies to the side of a plaza. If you head from the Plaza de España, following the road between the post office and Cabildo Insular, cross the *barranco* and turn right before reaching the barracks you enter the Plaza del Mercado and the market lies to the left. It is housed in a permanent building with a number of stalls spilling out onto the surrounding sidewalks and lanes. Everything has a price but haggling is an accepted form of purchase, particularly in the stalls selling goods other than fresh food. A little knowledge of Spanish is handy but not essential.

In February Santa Cruz hosts the carnival. This is a splendid event and it is said that only the carnival in Rio de Janiero is bigger. For a week the capital becomes a playground, music fills the air and the streets fill with colour. The highlight of the week is the grand procession — a cavalcade of floats, bands, dancers and entertainers. People come from all over the world and particularly from South America to take part, and salsa accompanies the procession as it follows the route along the dockside road and towards the Plaza de España. The plaza forms the centre piece of the theme chosen for the year. Recently King Kong was featured here, and the area has also been transformed into Egypt, complete with Sphinx and pyramids.

The cost of the carnival is enormous but such is the popularity of the event with tourists and residents alike that year after year the town council and government spend millions of pesetas to make each successive carnival bigger and better than the previous one. Top groups from South America, Spain and the islands hold concerts in the capital each night for the week of the carnival, and people dance in the streets to the vibrant beat of salsa. Fancy dress is almost compulsory and there seems to be no limit to the Canarians ingenious designs. Children are dressed in splendid, colourful costumes to dance and shuffle along in time to the music. Carnival time in Santa Cruz is a time for all the family and, like the capital itself, it is an experience that will long be remembered.

Additional Information

Places of Interest

Candelaria

Basilica de Candelaria
The Virgin Candelaria is the patron saint of the island. She resides in the basilica which is open to the public. Built in 1959 the church is modern but retains a colonial style, the plaza is guarded by ten statues of Guanches. Open: 7am-1pm and 3-7pm. ☎ 50 100

Santa Cruz de Tenerife

Museo Militar (Military Museum)
Calle de San Isidro
The cannon 'El Tigre' that was allegedly used when Nelson's arm was shot off is housed here, as well as other interesting artefacts such as the flags captured from Nelson. Open: 10am-2pm.
Closed Mondays. ☎ 27 16 72

Museo Municipal de Bellas Artes (Fine Arts Museum)
Calle José Murphy
A small but impressive art collection that is worth a visit.
Open: 2-8pm, Monday to Friday.
☎ 24 43 58

Museo Arqueologico (Archaeological Museum)
Plaza de España
An excellent museum that houses many ancient artefacts from the Guanche era. There are mummified bodies, skulls, pottery etc. In addition, there are displays using lifesize models to show how the ancient inhabitants lived.
Open: 9am-1pm and 4-6pm, Monday to Friday. Saturday 9am-1pm.
☎ 60 55 74

Palacio Carta
Plaza de Candelaria
This building dates from 1742 and is a superb example of the architecture of this period. It now houses a bank but visitors are welcome to look inside.
Open: 9am-2pm.

Iglesia de Nuestra Señora de la Concepcion
A fine church which is the capital's oldest (1502). It has recently been extensively refurbished but is closed. It is still worth a visit to see its exterior.

Tourist Information Centre

Santa Cruz

Plaza Espána
Open: Monday to Friday and Saturday.
☎ 60 55 92

3

THE ANAGA

T he Anaga is one of Tenerife's least visited areas but certainly one of her most beautiful. This region includes the areas east of Santa Cruz in the south and Tacoronte in the north, it therefore also takes in routes across the island that avoid Santa Cruz and *autopistas*. The Anaga, like the western part of the island, is mountainous and spectacular. There are a number of isolated villages and some charming coastal resorts, all of which seem locked in a time warp, only granting the advance of tourism cursory acknowledgement.

The mountain range that occupies the north-eastern end of the island is a wonderland of spectacular scenery, quiet beaches and abundant colour. It has a character so different from the remainder of Tenerife that it is possible to understand why many believe that at one time the area was a separate island.

When the Spanish arrived in Tenerife, the Guanches were camped to the west of the beach near Santa Cruz on which the landing took place. Had the Guanches been able to draw the Spanish east into the interior of the Anaga, there is every possibility the natives would have inflicted even greater damage and loss on the invaders. A guerilla war can drain the most well equipped army and, in the harsh interior of the Anaga range, there is little doubt the Guanches would have fared better.

There is a road system around the region, the tarmac following the old mule and donkey routes up, down and around the mountains. The roads are often in excellent condition, some are less than 10 years old. Even now many villages are only accessible on foot or by donkey, and those who make the journey down these roads often find that the way in is also the way out.

The Anaga is without doubt one of the most beautiful areas in

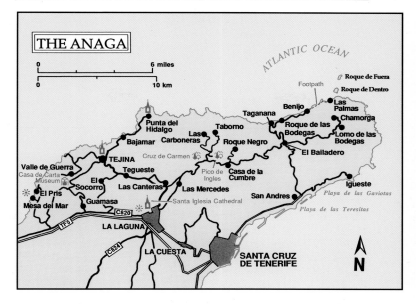

THE ANAGA

ATLANTIC OCEAN

0 ————— 6 miles
0 ————— 10 km

Footpath

Roque de Fuera
Roque de Dentro

Benijo
Taganana
Las Palmas
Chamorga
Punta del Hidalgo
Taborno
Roque de las Bodegas
Lomo de las Bodegas
Bajamar
Las Carboneras
Roque Negro
El Bailadero
Cruz de Carmen
Valle de Guerra
TEJINA
Casa de Carta Museum
Tegueste
Pico de Ingles
Casa de la Cumbre
El Socorro
Las Canteras
Las Mercedes
El Pris
Guamasa
Igueste
Mesa del Mar
Santa Iglesia Cathedral
San Andres
Playa de las Gaviotas
Playa de las Teresitas
C820
LA LAGUNA
TF-5
C824
LA CUESTA
SANTA CRUZ DE TENERIFE

N

Tenerife. All the roads can be covered in one day without any great hurry but there is so much to see and do that many will want to return to discover the beaches, enjoy the views and absorb more of this delightful region. There are a number of entry and exit points but, in keeping with the pattern of the book, we will enter from the south. Follow the road alongside the port in Santa Cruz past the Plaza de España and, keeping the port on your right, follow the traffic system that leads out of the city. You will arrive at a traffic light controlled junction with a Cepsa filling station on the left. It is worth noting that filling stations are few and far between in the Anaga and it is best to enter the region with a full tank of fuel. Continue straight on; 300m (330yd) beyond the junction is a small viewing point where cannons point to the sea. Although silent now, these artillery pieces once guarded the port.

Santa Cruz port is a series of harbours, quays and docks that stretch along the coastline for many kilometres. As you continue you pass the oil and fuel storage facilities where large crude tankers dock here in the deep water to unload the island's vital fuel. The few remaining fishing vessels lie alongside the pleasure boats in the marina, protected from the open sea by a huge artificial breakwater. Those interested in maritime matters will be interested in the large ships that have been hauled onto the quayside. Some of these ships are fascinating, such as the old steamers that plied their way between the islands before being made redundant by the aeroplane.

After the port facilities end, you soon enter the coastal town of San Andres. The road up into the hills is at the entrance of the town by the Mobil filling station. However, 6km (4 miles) further along the coastal road from the Cepsa Station, you will see the sign for **Playa de las Teresitas**. This beach is one of the best in the Canary Islands and yet, with the exception of Sundays, Bank Holidays and the holiday season of July, August and September, you are likely to find it almost deserted. Teresitas is an artificial paradise of imported, golden Sahara sand, protected from erosion by breakwaters and groynes. The beach stretches east for 2km (1 mile), backed by the towering hills and mountains of the Anaga. There is ample parking behind the beach and a number of bars are conveniently placed so that you can quench your thirst and take advantage of the shade. Because the beach is man-made, there are a number of facilities that the authorities have provided for visitors. Apart from the parking and bars, showers have been built at the rear of the beach. Palm trees and rush umbrellas are placed along the way to provide shade from the heat. Although Teresitas is man-made, it remains one of Tenerife's beauty spots.

At the entrance to the beach is a traffic light controlled junction. To the right is the entrance to Teresitas, whereas carrying straight on will lead you to the town of Igueste. The road climbs up away from the beach and soon you can stop to look back over the port and the golden sweep of Teresitas. After $3^1/_2$km (2 miles) there is an entrance signposted **Playa de las Gaviotas**. By turning down you will quickly descend to the coast and to a quiet and delightful beach. The azure waters lap at the black sand, and it is hard to imagine that just around the headland lies the port and capital. The beach is ideal for quiet family outings but there are no facilities or refreshments so take food and drink with you.

There are a number of other beaches along the coast but access to them can be difficult. For those who wish to explore, it is best to walk east from Playa de las Gaviotas. The 'main' road runs parallel to the coast before arriving in **Igueste** after 7km ($4^1/_2$ miles). This small rural village is as far as it is possible to go in a vehicle. Built either side of a lush *barranco*, the village can be seen spreading away from the road which seems to be the only one in the village — residents park on the main street and walk up to their houses. By following the road to the other side of the *barranco* you can park and walk beyond the end of the road down a wide footpath to the church, and beyond are a number of paths that are well marked and lead around the hill to the coast. As you return to Santa Cruz the views that can so easily be missed driving east are now clearly visible; the steep rising slopes, the craggy coastline, and sheer spits of lava that fall to the sea.

The Road into the Interior

There is only one road that allows access to the Anaga east of Santa Cruz. **San Andres** has developed since the building of the beach but retains many of the characteristics of a Canarian village. It is unusual for being dependent on both agriculture and fishing — evidence of both can be seen. By turning away from the coast at the Mobil station, you follow the road through the centre of the village.

Once over the stone bridge crossing the *barranco*, the track climbs quickly to leave the village behind, and very soon the Anaga comes into view. You climb through the floor of the valley and up through some of the richest land on the island. The hills and mountains fold like waves in the distance, a land of greenery made more spectacular by the contours of the rolling countryside. Spurs of land tumble away from the peaks falling to the valley floor. After $9^1/_2$km (6 miles) there is a junction, signposted to Taganana and Benijo. As you climb or descend it is worth noting that this seemingly remote area is well tended. Indeed, if you arrive in the early morning or the start of the siesta, you join the procession of farm vehicles that use the road.

The beauty of the road structure in the Anaga is that although many of the roads are dead ends, there is as much to see going in one direction as on the return journey. That is certainly true of the road to Taganana. Many maps will show the road as having an exit but the locals will advise against it. From the junction the road cuts through the mountain, the tunnel literally forming a gateway between north and south. To the south the views are of the valley and down to San Andres.

On emerging from the tunnel, Taganana and the northern coast are below you. The terraces climb the sometimes sheer sides of the mountain, and the houses of Taganana cling to the slopes, splashes of white rising from the valley floor. About 2km (1 mile) from the junction is a breathtaking viewpoint. Such are the contours of the land that views appear and disappear quickly between the peaks and escarpments.

From here the small islands off Tenerife's north-east coast become visible for the first time. The Roque de Dentro and the Roque de Fuera are evidence of the violent formation of the region; at 178m

The mile-long golden beach at Playa de las Teresitas is probably the best in the Canary Islands

(584ft) and 64m (210ft) respectively, their sheer sides are constantly battered by wind and sea.

After 4¹/₂km (2¹/₂ miles) you enter **Taganana**. The village rises from the main road and the entrance is signposted, leading to a series of houses built on the steep slopes divided by narrow lanes. At the foot of the valley the land around the village is abundant with vines, maize, potatoes and other plants that grow in the shadow of the hills and the solitary peak of Roque de las Animas at 373m (1,223ft). The *barranco* is a source of water and the greenest plants are to be seen sprouting from the often water-filled bed.

The road drops quickly to the coast, from high above the surf looks far rougher than it actually is, the isolated rocks of lava in the sea are circled with the white foam as the sea crashes through the narrow channels between them. After 7km (4¹/₂ miles) you enter the coastal village of **Roque de las Bodegas**. There is a small beach, and a mixture of sand and pebbles with low surf. A few bars and restaurants are to be found, the fishermen that fish from the rocky coast can be seen taking refreshment to wash away the taste of the salt spray.

If you choose a day of high winds the spectacle here can be awe-inspiring, with the sea crashing into the exposed rocks hurling plumes of spray high over the beach and promenade. There is little danger here but further along the road you are warned about the dangerous currents that swirl under the seemingly placid waters of the beach before Benijo. The beach is marked on many maps as a safe place for swimming, indeed many people ignore the notices and ride the surf. A small bar has been established here and the beach is pleasant enough to lie and top up the tan. However, the currents are strong and the warnings should be heeded.

Benijo is the end of the road. The track climbs away from the beach and enters this small, quaint village. As you reach the no entry sign there is a small bar at which you will be made welcome as the villagers are very friendly. The tarmac has only been laid for 10 years and many of the villagers still recall the treks to Taganana and over the hills to Santa Cruz. From here you can walk the paths that cross the fertile soil and towards the coast. Here, at the very tip of Tenerife, time stands still. Agriculture forms the basis of the community's income and potatoes, maize and vines are grown in the rich soil. It is difficult to see why a community was founded here at all, for little evidence of the fishing trade remains and before the road was laid it must have been hard for farmers to get their crops to market.

Benijo is where the road ends, but your journey may continue. On the north-eastern tip of Tenerife a number of villages lay hidden from view by the peaks and cut off from the island other than by footpaths. One such village, **Las Palmas**, is a brisk 5km (3 miles) walk from Benijo. It is one of the least accessible parts of the island but surely one of the most beautiful; a collection of small houses, a church and views of the eastern coast that defy description. It is a wonderful place and well worth the walk. From Benijo it is also possible to walk to Chamorga.

Going back to the road from San Andres into the interior, turn right. Two kilometres (1 mile) further on, the road reaches another junction. Turn left and the road returns to La Laguna. Turn right and you drive along a crest towards the village of Chamorga. Your views will depend on the weather, but below are the deep valleys leading to the coast. If it is a cloudy day you may well find you experience the unnerving sight of clouds running up the side of the valley and over the road. The swirling white mist, pushed by the thermals and wind from the valley floor, climbs up over the road to leave a white tunnel through which you drive. It spoils the view but is a unique and fascinating experience.

On a clear day there is a panorama of rolling hills and high peaks. The road is narrow and twists through hills, and after $4^1/_2$km ($2^1/_2$ miles) there is a small park with a barbecue area. Signposts indicate walks that can be taken through the trees to capture the views beyond. After 6km (4 miles) there is a lay-by from where the view of the southern valley can be enjoyed to the full. This is wild country, where the harsh terrain has been tamed only by the fortitude and considerable skill of the scattered inhabitants over many generations.

There are two villages at the end of the road, now a single track that only widens at the frequent bends. About 10km (6 miles) down this track is a junction. Turning left takes you through a short, roughly-hewn tunnel to Chamorga. Beyond the tunnel the road drops steeply to the village in the valley. An oasis nestling in the valley, **Chamorga** is a small collection of neat houses, spread across a valley floor dotted with palms. The *fincas* are neat and productive and there is, of course, a small bar. Beyond the village, reached only on foot, is the lighthouse that sits on top of the peninsular. This unspoilt corner of Tenerife lures walkers from far and wide.

From the junction you can also reach **Lomo de las Bodegas**. This close-knit community sits high on a plateau above the valley, a fragile collection of small houses with palms adding a tropical touch to the surrounding farmland.

From the junctions to Taganana and Chamorga the road leads

towards La Laguna. **Casa de la Cumbre** is a hamlet that stretches for 2km (1 mile) along the road. Astride the crest, the houses enjoy views to the coast below. To the south the countryside is a harsh terrain of mountains and hills, but a few seemingly inaccessible villages appear in the deep gorges. To the north the terrain is no less rugged but there are a number of hamlets and villages that can be reached, though most are accessible only on foot or in all-terrain vehicles.

About 7km (4^1/$_2$ miles) from the last junction there is a brief excursion into the valley and to the hamlet of **Roque Negro**. This, like many of the inhabited sites, is centred around the church but there are many other dwellings that use the name of the village as an address and yet are more than a few kilometres away, visible as faint white specks clinging to the hillside.

The main road continues along the ridge, at nearly 1,000m (3,300ft) above sea level. Whatever the weather, the effects of the elements on the view can be considerable. On days of high cloud the sun throws moving shadows onto the land below and the green of the landscape seems to change hue as the cloud passes. On days of extreme heat the ground shimmers in a mirage-induced dance. In winter, frost glistens in the early morning before the sun rises to leave the plants dew-heavy. Early morning is a very special time in the Anaga. An early start is essential because the sight of the sun rising from the sea to climb behind the mountains is an unforgettable experience.

Las Carboneras and **Taborno** lie in the northern valleys, below the main road. The entrance to the villages is via a narrow lane that leads for 9km (5^1/$_2$ miles) off the main road. The valley is steep, as you drop down on the track there is another junction, after 3km (2 miles), where the road divides to follow separate routes either side of the valley to the two villages. Las Carboneras and Taborno face each other in the shadow of the peak of the Rock of Taborno at 706m (2,315ft). They are only joined across the valley by a footpath. Both villages are similar in size, a number of tidy houses from which the *fincas* spread along the valley. As always, there are bars and it is perhaps worth noting that to the inhabitants the bar is far more than a place to enjoy the local wine or other liquid refreshment. Admittedly their importance to the community stems from the fact that most of the male inhabitants are regular visitors. With the communities so well spread out and in some cases inaccessible, the bar takes on a number of other functions. The council will post notices regarding every aspect of local life, such as rates and changes in law, knowing that almost all the village will see them. The postman leaves post for the far houses, knowing that it will be collected or passed on.

Continuing along the main route there is another junction. Turn left, and within 1km ($^1/_2$ mile) the road enters a roundabout before going back on itself. Park here, for the **Pico de Ingles** (Englishmen's Peak) is one of the most impressive viewpoints in Tenerife. The views open up on three sides. High on a prominent ridge the *mirador* enjoys views across the Anaga and beyond. The green-coated valley lies below, and the road can be seen twisting through the trees. From this altitude you can appreciate how lush and yet how barren the area can be. The granite towers rise up from the abundant valley floors, sheer craggy pillars of stone on which no plant can gain a foothold. At the side of the restaurant is a path that leads to the highest part of the peak. From here Teide can be seen rising alone in the distance, while the apartment blocks of Hidalgo are no more than matchboxes on the rugged coast of the horizon.

Having climbed from the road through the forests to Pico Ingles, you now descend through the woods to the plains that surround La Laguna. Returning to the junction, carry straight on and the road emerges at the Cruz de Carmen. At a height of 920m (3,018ft) the *mirador* provides some delightful panoramas of the valley below and beyond across to Esperanza and Teide. About 500m (1,640ft) beyond the *mirador* is a turning to El Batán and El Moquinal. The twisting track leads high into the hills, arriving at the small village of El Batán.

The road begins to drop fast here, the gradient is steep and the *fincas* are terraced. Occasionally through the trees the view reveals a solitary house standing in the centre of the productive land. Another *mirador* (Mirador de Aguere) sits on a bend, and from lower down the details of the valley are easier to define. The spires of La Laguna can be distinguished, proud over the closely-built streets and houses. After about another 4km ($2^1/_2$ miles) you reach Las Mercedes (La Laguna is signposted to the left).

The Anaga can be entered from **La Laguna**, the cultural, religious and learning centre of Tenerife. One of the oldest inhabited sites on the island, the town is a mixture of established colonial buildings and modern shops and offices. If you leave the *autopista* at Junction 6 and follow the signs for La Laguna you will, if approaching from the south, go through a series of crossroads, at all of which you have right of way. You run parallel to the *autopista* before rising to the junction — turn right and you enter the town. The statue on top of the junction on the western side is of the friar Anchieta. Born in La Laguna, the friar went to South America and, it is said, converted many of the natives of the New World to Christianity. The statue was a gift to the island from the people of Brazil.

The university is located on the outskirts of the town, close to the *autopista*. This is the university for the whole archipelago, and plans to build another in Gran Canaria have met stiff opposition. Many subjects are taught here and the university enjoys a good reputation for training students to a high standard. As you enter the town, look for the signs to Bajamar and Las Mercedes, turn left and then, following the same signs, turn right, follow the narrow streets past the cathedral and out of the town, down the leafy lanes to the junction at Las Canteras.

It is worthwhile spending time in La Laguna, a town of considerable charm and immense history. As you turn left for Bajamar, park in the quiet road near the old, low church. The road that leads off here to Bajamar will lead you into the heart of the old town and to the Santa Iglesia cathedral. This is built in a small square and unfortunately it is impossible to stand back from the cathedral to view the impressive building to full advantage. The church was consecrated in 1913 and is far more impressive on the inside than the outside, where the views of the building are restricted by the closeness of the shops. Unlit except for the sun and the flickering candles by the altar, the cathedral has a serene atmosphere. Whereas many of the great churches of Europe have been turned into tourist attractions, the only concessions to modernity are the speakers discreetly mounted high on the giant columns inside. The interior is a mixture of Gothic and Baroque. The Gothic influence is clearly seen in the presbytery with its pointed arches and in the decorated windows of the east end.

The altar stands alone at the end of the twin naves, adorned with flowers. To the right is the Virgin, her innocent face reflecting the colours of the burnished gold that surrounds her. In the treasury, for a small entrance fee, you can see the painted figures that are carried in the Christmas, Easter and Corpus Christi processions. The cathedral remains an active place of worship, so accordingly access may be restricted for those who just wish to visit.

The main shopping centre is located between the cathedral and the main road by which you entered the town. While you are shopping, keep an eye above street level for the intricate balconies that protrude from the older houses.

On the day of Corpus Christi, many of the streets of La Laguna are closed to traffic. The streets are bedecked with flowers, which are spread on the road in the most attractive and complicated patterns. Together with La Orotava, La Laguna is one of the principal sites for this important religious festival.

Before you enter the interior of the Anaga from La Laguna, there is a route into the capital that has much to offer and which also avoids the congestion of the *autopista*. At the junction of the road leading from the centre of the town with the *autopista*, follow the signs to La Cuesta. After $1^1/_2$km (1 mile) turn left into the narrow road signposted Los Campitos. Soon after leaving the town the road narrows and climbs, and the views of the gorge open as you enter the hamlet of Valle Jimenez, 3km (2 miles) away. Santa Cruz can be seen through the open end of the *barranco*. Still climbing, the route passes the terraces and after 6km (4 miles) comes into Los Campitos.

As you descend past the enormous reservoir, Santa Cruz harbour can be seen below, and, after just over 8km (5 miles) there is a lay-by from which the capital can be viewed, laid in front of you so that buildings and parks, squares and churches can be picked out. The port is clearly visible and at night the lights of the harbour reflect on the still waters of the basins. After dark, Santa Cruz takes on another guise and from the *mirador* high above the lights, the bustle of the capital is in sharp contrast to the silence of the viewpoint. The road enters the city just after 10km (6 miles). Turn left at the T junction and enter the city, or turn right and you rejoin the northern *autopista*.

The area that lies to the north and north-west of La Laguna is distinctly different from the region eastwards. Leaving the town towards Las Mercedes the view is of grass fields, only the mountains that rise in the distance give a hint of the rugged interior. Three kilometres (2 miles) from the last buildings of La Laguna, you enter the small village of Las Canteras. Turn right at the junction and the route follows the road through Las Mercedes and into the Anaga. By continuing on the main route you travel along the valley floor, green with plants and trees.

Tegueste is a modern village, spread out across the base of the valley. Villas stand in neat rows and walled gardens show a variety of colourful plants and shrubs. Beyond Tegueste is a turning, $4^1/_2$km (3 miles) from Las Canteras, to El Socorro. The road continues through the productive countryside to **Tejina**, an important commercial centre situated at the bridging point of a deep *barranco* and a junction of two busy roads. To approach the coast follow the signs to Bajamar.

The coast from Tacoronte to Punta del Hildalgo has few beaches but, to compensate for this, swimming pools using the natural coastline have been built. **Bajamar** is one such resort. The road from Tejina loops around the *barranco* and down to the coast. You enter Bajamar and after about 3km (2 miles) the Piscinas Municipales

The Santa Iglesia cathedral in La Laguna has an impressive Gothic and Baroque interior

Las Mercedes lies in a lush, green rolling valley

them. There is a delightful atmosphere at the sea front, although there never seem to be great crowds of people. Car parking is easy and the bars and restaurants always have space. The place can be busy but never becomes crowded. The pools back onto a small shingle beach, and are large and clean, filled with seawater and surrounded by ample terracing for sunbathing. In August there is a festival in honour of Cristo del Gran Poder, including fun fairs and fireworks. Along the coast are algae-coated rocks from where fishermen cast into the low surf. A paved walkway along the shoreline completes the picture. A recent programme of refurbishment has seen a great deal of investment in the future of Bajamar. The sea shore pools are being refitted and the resort is regaining some of its old self. Bajamar is a resort that seems to be waiting for the crowds, but for now you can enjoy a tranquillity broken only by the roar of the surf.

Punta del Hidalgo has been developed more than Bajamar, but even so it remains a sleepy resort. By continuing along the main road through the village you arrive at a *mirador*. Below the countryside is rugged, and rocks stand in isolation in the waves, while bananas are grown almost down to the seashore. Ahead are the mountains of the Anaga around which the coast continues. As you head back into the town, just beyond the unusual red church, there is a turning signposted for the swimming pools (*piscinas*). The road drops to the coast, and in front are the pools. Turn right at the end, by the side of the apartments, where the road becomes a track which is rough in places but passable. It follows a dusty route along the coastline. The lava has flowed to the sea to cool into a plateau of rock pools, and there are flat areas of sand that can be your private beach for sunbathing. Children fish with nets in the pools for fish trapped by the retreating tide, while the adults cast from rocks close to the sea. The track peters to a path after 2km (1 mile) and this follows the shore around the cliff and headland.

There are a number of hotels in Hidalgo but the resort, like Bajamar, remains relatively untouched by the advance of tourism. If you visit the coast here you will obviously hope for good weather, but bad weather has the advantage of providing a spectacle of roaring seas that smash across the rocks and against the cliffs.

As you return to Tejina, the one way system takes you past the church. With its two steeples, one old and one new, the church stands in a large plaza. Tejina's shopping centre is grouped around the church and can provide a pleasant distraction.

Turning back onto the main road will take you to the next village, **Valle de Guerra**, 2½ km (1 mile) from Tejina. This large village lies inland. After sweeping along the top of the coastal plain, the road reaches this bustling agricultural centre. The Casa de Carta Museum is a preserved eighteenth-century house which gives an insight into life in Tenerife at that time. At the end of the village you can turn down towards the coastal area of El Pris and Mesa del Mar. The famous 'Bird of Paradise' flower, the *strelizia*, is grown in abundance in Valle de Guerra and the wealth it brings the area is obvious. Large villas and haciendas are situated in the middle of the *fincas* and their gardens are splendid. The road begins to climb steeply and below one can see the coastal *fincas* of bananas and flowers.

About 6km (4 miles) from Tejina is a junction that will lead you back to the *autopista*. If you intend to rejoin the *autopista*, this route is one of the prettiest by which to do so. For 5km (3 miles) the road leads up, twisting through the green contours of the climb. All the while the view to the coast below opens up, in the distance the villages of Tejina and Tegueste can be seen, closer is Valle de Guerra. The road emerges onto the old northern road opposite the junction for the Golf Club and Agua Garcia.

If you wish to continue on the road between Valle de Guerra and Tacoronte, take the turning signposted El Pris, 3½ km (2 miles) after the junction to Guamasa.

El Pris and Mesa del Mar are typical of the many coastal towns and villages around Tenerife that are waiting to fulfil their potential. The road that loops from just outside Tacoronte to Valle de Guerra descends from the inland road. About 2½ km (1 mile) from the junction you approach a crossroads, turn left and the road goes past some neat bungalows and then descends. From the heights **Mesa del Mar** can be seen in a small quiet bay. A large hotel sits on the headland, and to the side of the hotel are a number of swimming pools. They normally hold salt water and are very pleasant.

The road descends quickly, and within 2km (1 mile) you reach the resort itself. Mesa del Mar is one of the most haunting resorts in Tenerife. The large apart hotel, now nearly thirty years old, is threatened with demolition. The local authority wish to put a foot-path across the coast and the hotel is in the way. A shame for those who invested in this building just when Tenerife was opening as a holiday destination. Still the resort retains that wonderful feeling of escapism. The restaurants open and close as they want to, the tunnel to the beach is often open but then is also often closed! Through the tunnel is access to a large and well sheltered beach. There is also a new restaurant and one assumes further facilities are planned. Pedestrian access to the beach is unrestricted. A gentle breeze floats

The panoramic view from above Valle de Guerra

The Casa de Carta Museum houses artifacts from the eighteenth century

A traditional shuttered window at the Casa de Carta Museum

across the bay to cool the heat of the midday sun and yet it seems to be waiting for something to happen.

The resort has plenty of interest and there are no crowds. One particular attraction is the small chapel, which is always open. The building is very small and, when full of flowers, it is impossible to imagine any more than three people fitting inside. You enter and leave the resort via a one way system. Coming down to the resort you will notice the concrete quays which are ideal for sunbathing and there are small rock pool and swimming pools in which you can cool off. Mesa del Mar is very much a resort that has suffered from the opening of the south but it retains a warm, friendly feeling and is well worth a visit.

About 2km (1 mile) beyond the crossroads is the entrance to **El Pris**. You can walk between here and Mesa del Mar, along the ragged coastline and seashore. El Pris, like its neighbour, seems not so much neglected as in need of investment. There is a small but pleasing beach onto which the tide softly rolls through the offshore islets of lava, quietened by a harbour wall from which the local children dive and fish. The Canarian flag stands proudly above the biggest islet, a pillar of lava that rises from the sea. A few apartments have been constructed here but it remains a quiet and tranquil resort, and it is perhaps best left as such. Leave El Pris by the same road you entered. If you turn left at the junction, the road continues for 3½km (2 miles) and leads to Valle de Guerra.

Additional Information

Places of Interest

La Laguna

Santa Iglesia Cathedral
A splendid sixteenth-century building with twentieth-century additions in the dome and twin towers. The virgin is situated to the right of the nave and the tomb of Alonso de Lugo, conqueror of the islands, is behind the ornate altar. This church is the religious centre of Tenerife.

Iglesia de Nuestra Señora de la Concepcion
This church dates from 1502 and is one of the oldest churches in Tenerife. The font dates from Guanche times when the conquered leaders were baptised here.

Valle de Guerra

Casa de Carta Museum
The Casa de Carta is an eighteenth-century rural house. Set in splendid gardens, it houses a collection of traditional costumes as well as everyday items used in days gone by. Of particular interest is the kitchen where the room is preserved as it would have been centuries ago. Open: 10am-1pm and 3-6pm winter. In summer the afternoon opening times are 4-7pm. Closed Fridays.

4

NORTHERN TENERIFE

T he north of the island was the first to see tourism as a future source of income. Even today the oldest resort of Puerto de la Cruz has a feel of tradition that has survived through the vast building programmes. The north is very green — you notice it immediately, a green carpet of flora and foliage that makes this area so attractive. Climb away from the coast, and look back across valleys where only the white of the houses and the red of the roofs interrupt the verdant slopes that flow to the sea. The north has a number of large towns, all of which have the tradition of the island indelibly written on their character.

Northern Tenerife can be said to stretch from the wilderness beyond Punta Hidalgo in the east to Punta Teno in the west. This chapter describes the area to the west of Tacoronte, and the route follows the island road as far as Icod and heads inland as far as Orotava. The area is one of history and tradition, for it was here that the invading Spanish finally conquered the Guanches. It was also here that tourism first made an impression on the islanders' way of life. When you compare the north with the south you realise how very different the two region's weather, vegetation, architecture and pace of life are. There are long established towns such as La Orotava and La Victoria who have history written in every nook and cranny, resorts such as Puerto de la Cruz which, despite the advance of tourism, retain a certain character that the southern counterparts cannot equal, and inland villages that nestle amongst the lush vegetation and verdant slopes of the hills.

We will start our journey along this part of the northern coast from **Tacoronte**. This important market town can be approached from three directions. Firstly along the northern *autopista*, by the old road

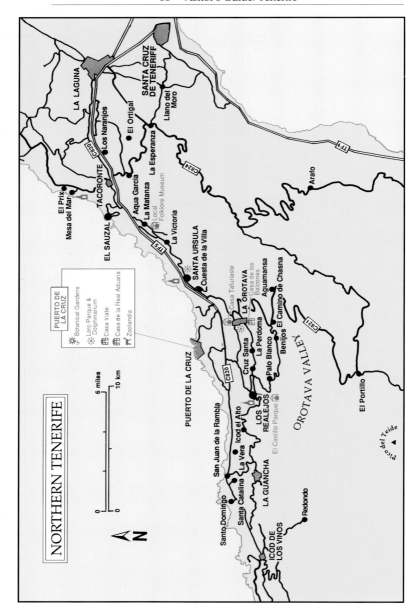

The church at El Sauzal

El Sauzal has a number of exclusive villas

that runs parallel to the motorway from La Laguna; secondly from La Esperanza and Agua Garcia in the interior; and thirdly, one can also approach from the coastal road from Valle de Guerra and Mesa del Mar. From Tacoronte the main island route continues first as *autopista* and later as a single carriageway to Icod. Unlike the southern *autopista*, many of the junctions are unnumbered, so a keen eye should be kept open. One can reach Icod without using the *autopista* and main island road at all, and that is the route described below.

The approach to Tacoronte from the hills above the town, reveals how different the north and south of the island really are. At La Esperanza it is like entering another country; gone is the parched desert of the south and in its place is a rich, fertile land. The north, away from the coast, is a verdant land of trees, crops and plants. In Tacoronte you first meet the junction leading to Valle de Guerra. As you head through the busy streets, it is worth noting that in the past this town was linked to Santa Cruz by a tramway. Many of today's commuters who drive into Santa Cruz would, in days gone by, have enjoyed a leisurely ride.

After leaving Tacoronte you can either rejoin the *autopista* or head along the old route towards the coastal village of **El Sauzal**, the entrance to which is $4^1/_2$km ($2^1/_2$ miles) beyond the *autopista* junction. El Sauzal lies below the main road. Perched on the steep rise from the sea are a number of exclusive villas and developments. You can drive along the tree-lined road and admire the superb views across the bay to Puerto de la Cruz in the distance. By turning right by the church, you follow the road down and along a ridge through well-tended *fincas* and gardens. The road is quiet, so normally there is the opportunity to pull over and admire the panoramic view. After 3km (2 miles) is the turning that leads to the sea, or by carrying on past the developments of La Primavera and Los Perales, you emerge next to the northern *autopista* below La Matanza, just over $4^1/_2$km ($2^1/_2$ miles) away. El Sauzal itself is a pleasing and open town and, while much of the surrounding area is dominated by villas, it retains a homely and unspoilt feel.

La Matanza (The Massacre) and nearby La Victoria (The Victory) are the sites of the conflicts between the invading Spanish and native Guanches. Today both are peaceful market towns. La Victoria can be reached by turning right and following the road alongside the *autopista*. **La Matanza** is approached by crossing over the bridge and climbing up above the motorway. On entering the town you will see the local museum advertised; this lies behind the main road and is worth a visit. About $2^1/_2$km ($1^1/_2$ miles) after crossing the motorway there is a junction; turn left and you enter the heart of the town. The museum is $1^1/_2$km (1 mile) up this road on the right. Inside are a number of displays concerning the history of the area and local products and handiwork. This road continues up into the hills and into a system of lanes and tracks. To explore them, it is best to return to Agua Garcia.

As you head down from La Esperanza, turning right at the T junction will lead to the *autopista* near Tacoronte. If you turn left the route leads to La Matanza. After about 2km (1 mile) the hamlet of San Cristobal has a junction that allows a quick drop into La Matanza after $5^1/_2$km ($3^1/_2$ miles). As the road drops, note the pink church on the junction after 700m (760yd), carry straight on and over the next small crossroads, and you enter La Matanza above the museum.

At San Cristobal you can also head straight on. The route takes you through the spread out *fincas* and homesteads above La Matanza. After passing the small church there is a turning 3km (2 miles) later, carry straight on and you soon reach a crossroads. Turn left and the road soon becomes a track, turn right and you rejoin the road from San Cristobal to La Matanza. Alternatively, you can carry straight on and edge through *fincas* of vines, potatoes and chestnut trees until you reach another junction after 5km (3 miles). Turn right and head down, after a further 500m (550yd) keep to the 'main' road and continue past traditional houses until you reach the crossroads after about 6km (4 miles). Carry straight on again and after another 6km (4 miles) turn left at the crossroads. This road is the same one that leads from La Matanza to San Cristobal and you enter the town after $2^1/_2$km ($1^1/_2$ miles).

From La Matanza the road to Icod leads to **La Victoria**. Like so many of the northern towns, La Victoria has a traditional feel. It has developed over the centuries through the established agricultural business and, while the region is aware that tourism is now an important part of the island's culture, little has or will change here. You enter the town 1km ($^1/_2$ mile) beyond the junction in La Matanza and you can travel through the tree-lined roads in peace. The high street has a good selection of shops and the banks and post office are here. The town spreads above and below the road which, as you leave the town, begins to wind down to the coast. After about $2^1/_2$km ($1^1/_2$ miles) is the access road that leads to and from the *autopista*. By staying on the inland route, the road carries on over the *barranco* and past a green canopy of trees and vines to Santa Ursula.

Santa Ursula is one of the prettiest towns in Tenerife. As people

Santa Ursula has pleasant tree-lined boulevards where you can relax

*Puerto de la Cruz from
Cuesta la Villa*

*The old part of La Orotava
has cobbled streets and
elegant architecture*

hurry by below, many look up and admire the town but few visit it. There are palms that line the wide boulevards, whitewashed buildings and wooden balconies and in the plaza is a delightful church. Having been established for many years, these towns are beyond the breezeblock stage and while building goes on, it somehow fails to detract from their inherent beauty and tradition.

As you descend, the *autopista* can occasionally be spotted through the trees. After about $6^1/_2$km (4 miles) there is yet another junction allowing access to the main route, and beyond that is the small village of Cuesta de la Villa. *Cuesta* is Spanish for slope, and by now the gradient is noticeable. Below, Puerto has appeared on the coast, and the impressive view of Teide lies before you. After about 7km ($4^1/_2$ miles) you reach the junction leading to La Orotava or to Icod. Take the right fork and the road drops 2km (1 mile) to the *autopista* above Puerto de la Cruz.

The Orotava Valley

The Orotava valley is one of the great remaining beauty spots of Tenerife. The green landscape is dotted with villas and homesteads, and the sheer verdant beauty of the area is breathtaking. By taking the left fork to La Orotava you soon reach a *mirador*. From here, high above the valley, you can look down on the plantations and across to Puerto resting on the coast. The road continues until, after 1km ($^1/_2$ mile), you approach the famous Mirador de Humboldt, named after the German naturalist who was so impressed with the beauty of the valley. It is well worth stopping here, although the tranquillity of the view is deceiving. Below, the industry of farming continues unabated, plantations of bananas spread along the valley floor. Above, pines can be seen in the hills, forming dense forests on the lower slopes of the island's interior. After 10km (6 miles) you enter La Orotava.

La Orotava is a large and very important town. As a junction it provides access to both the mountain and the coast. As a commercial centre it houses offices and the associated businesses for the agriculture carried on around it. It is best to view La Orotava on foot, for it is a town of parks, narrow streets and stately architecture. The old part of the town has cobbled streets — as you approach the fountain, drive up and to the right. The junction is signposted to Las Cañadas. If the mountain is your destination you can still view much of the town by carrying on into the modern centre. At the T junction turn left and follow the now cobbled surface past the palatial Town Hall. This is a good spot to park and explore, above the narrow streets whose houses, many of which date from the seventeenth century, have traditional wooden balconies.

Beyond the Town Hall, turn left and continue past La Casa del Balcones. Now a lace centre, this old property is worth exploring even if you are not buying. Inside is a courtyard which is green with plants and above are the intricate wooden balconies after which the building is named. If you continue past the Casa del Balcones, the road travels up, away from the centre. At the T junction the road to Las Canadas is to the left. This road is described on page 92. The inland route continues to the right.

Above the *autopista*, the often uneven but passable surface passes through the rural villages and hamlets. From La Perdoma, $2^1/_2$km ($1^1/_2$ miles) away, you can view the coast. The resorts below provide much of the work for the younger generations. After 4km ($2^1/_2$ miles), Cruz Santa is passed and after $4^1/_2$km ($2^1/_2$ miles) you reach a crossroads. By heading straight on you drive down, past the giant reservoir, to below Los Realejos, La Zamora is to the right. Turn left and the route continues inland to Los Realejos. After $^1/_2$km ($^1/_4$ mile) you approach the turning to Chasna at Palo Blanco and, $1^1/_2$km (1 mile) beyond that, you enter the top of **Los Realejos**.

This is a town that spreads over many square kilometres and on which the nearby resorts rely heavily. Much of the 'tourist' part of the town is below the main road but it is the higher parts that offer so much to see and do. Apart from agriculture, the town provides many of the support industries the resorts need. There is an excellent shopping centre which is centred around the plaza and interesting church, which is topped by an unusual tiled spire. As a resort Los Realejos lives in the shadow of Puerto de la Cruz but the nearby beach, Playa Socorro, is a pleasant site. Much of the older part of Los Realejos lies in the *barranco* that bisects the town and a brisk walk down alleys and narrow roads will always reveal something of interest. The road from the town to the *autopista* is well signposted at the junction and by following the road around by the church and Town Hall, you can turn left to continue along the inland route to Icod.

As you leave Los Realejos, agriculture is again the predominant occupation. The *barrancos*, slopes and foothills are terraced while scattered houses are occasionally visible in amongst the crops and orchards. After $4^1/_2$km ($2^1/_2$ miles) you reach **Icod el Alto**, high above the coast and giving unrivalled views to the sea. Icod el Alto is a small, content village where the pace of life seems slow but steady.

Once clear of the village the road begins to climb, after 8km (5 miles) you cross the *barranco* and climb along the cliff face. Below are *fincas* and terraces, and as you reach the zenith of the climb you are rewarded by the view across the valleys and plantations to Puerto and beyond. The sheer sides of the deep *barranco* are lined with pines, and from the *mirador* you can look down into the gorge that falls away vertically below. You pass through the sleepy hamlet of Las Rosas and, after about 11km (7 miles), you turn down to the right to rejoin the main island route at San Juan de la Rambla.

La Guancha is the main town on the route and owes its importance to the presence of the town council and the fact that Icod is nearby. In the centre of the town is another road to the *autopista* below. La Guancha is built either side of a *barranco*, and the older houses can be viewed from them main tree-lined way, nestling on the slopes below the town.

After $13^1/_2$km ($8^1/_2$ miles) is a *zona recreativa*, from here you can drive down to the main road. After $18^1/_2$km ($11^1/_2$ miles) the road descends to join the main island route just east of Icod.

Santa Cruz to Icod By the Main Road

The area surrounding Santa Cruz and the eastern tip of the island is described in Chapter 2. If you bypass the area and require a quick route then the northern *autopista* is designed to do just that. In order to reach our start point at Tacoronte, the road from the capital is described briefly here.

As you climb away from Santa Cruz, housing complexes, villages and industry continue close to the road while the foothills of the Anaga mountains can be seen in the distance. After $2^1/_2$km ($1^1/_2$ miles) is the entrance to Taco and just beyond that the entrance to La Cuesta. A brief excursion can be had here, if you follow the road through the industry of the town to the T junction, turn left and then right after 500m (550yd) at the signpost to Los Campitos, you can climb up to a *mirador* above the capital.

The junctions on the northern *autopista* are not always numbered, so a sharp eye should be kept open for the kilometre and 500m warning signs. You will also notice how the four lane motorway (on which lane discipline is non existent), becomes three lanes without a great deal of warning. The next junction allows access to a small village called Las Chumberas and $1^1/_2$km (1 mile) later the junction is to La Laguna. This junction and the next one allow access to the town, but the system is somewhat confusing for new visitors. Leave at the first junction but follow the signs to Las Cañadas. You have

A fun way for children to see the sights of Puerto de la Cruz

right of way, where the road goes under the bridge, over the filter road and then runs parallel with the autopista. Go up the exit ramp, turn right for La Laguna and left to enter the Portillo road to Teide. By entering the one way system one can join the old road that runs parallel to the *autopista*. The next junction leads to the old airport and it is here that it is easier to follow the old route westwards. The following sequence of junctions all lead to the old road or to the interior. At junction 11 you can leave the motorway and enter Tacoronte close to the turning for Valle de Guerra.

The road that pre-dates the *autopista* has much to commend it, not least of which is its fine selection of restaurants. The turnings along the way lead to the villages and towns described in the section of the book covering the Anaga (Chapter 3). By leaving the *autopista* at the old airport and turning away from the airport and then left, you run parallel to the motorway along a tree-lined route. After about $^1/_2$km ($^1/_4$ mile) is the road to El Socorro, and less than 1km ($^1/_2$ mile) later the junction to Guamasa. The road inland to Agua Garcia is followed after 5km (3 miles) by the road to Valle de Guerra and soon after is the sleepy village of Los Naranjeros. Tacoronte lies at the end of the road. The route is not as fast as the *autopista* but infinitely more interesting.

From Tacoronte the dual carriageway of the *autopista* cuts its way through the green heartland of the north. The best views are often inland, where the villages that nestle in the hills and slopes can be seen. About $1^1/_2$km (1 mile) after the second junction to Tacoronte is the junction to El Sauzal, followed almost immediately by the exit to La Matanza. Santa Ursula is next, about 4km ($2^1/_2$ miles) beyond La Matanza. The road requires concentration so is best not taken if you are not in a hurry and want to admire the views. The junction to La Quinta arrives almost unannounced as it is only 700m (760yd) after the previous exit. The first junction to Orotava is 1km ($^1/_2$ mile) beyond here and soon after the road narrows to a single lane. For those wishing to continue west, the left hand lane is signposted Icod, and the right hand lane leads into Puerto de la Cruz.

✳ PUERTO DE LA CRUZ

Puerto, as it is more familiarly known, is a port whose importance as a harbour has been eclipsed by its place as the island's longest established and most traditional tourist resort. Unlike the southern resorts, Puerto existed long before the tourist industry boomed and, as you wander through the streets, it is possible to admire the older houses and buildings that give the port and resort such character.

Puerto, despite the new competition from the south, remains one of the premier resorts in the Canaries, the superb lido and the small but pleasant beach add to the charm of the resort and enhance its character.

Puerto has three entrances. The first one that you encounter, as the *autopista* divides, leads down towards the lidos. By following the signs for 'Botanico' you reach the Botanical Gardens. The walled, sub-tropical gardens have been established for centuries. As you wander through the canopies of green, the variety and beauty of the plants, trees and shrubs from all over the world will astound you. There are palms from California grown next to shrubs from Brazil, and the different colours of the flowers are almost infinite.

From here the road drops into the heart of the resort. By parking in one of the many side streets, you can head down to the coast and to the famous lidos. Not having a large beach, Puerto's man-made lidos more than suffice. For a minimal charge, you can enter a complex of pools. There are changing facilities, bars and cafés in the area, which includes a number of pools, some sea water and some freshwater. Between are paved promenades where the visitors lie and soak up the sun.

A promenade leads along the sea front to the older part of the port. Fishermen still haul in their catches here and will take no objection to you watching them go about their daily work. Puerto used to have a promenade market, and local crafts are still sold from stalls. Local artists paint in oil, crayon and chalk. Many of the works are excellent and prices very reasonable; some of the artists will, for a price, preserve your tan for posterity by painting your portrait. This is now situated away from the main tourist area in San Felipe but is still worth a visit.

The heart of Puerto, centred around the plaza and church, is a network of alleys, cobbled roads and walkways. At the corners and junctions, small squares lie in the shade. You are likely to find a streetside café, where explorers quench their thirst before continuing onwards. There is much to see and much to do; Puerto has something for everyone.

The town can be entered from other junctions further along the main island road, now a single carriageway. About 1km ($^1/_2$ mile) after the entrance to the resort is a junction that will lead up to La Orotava, passing the Bananera el Guanche which is open to the public. This is a commercial banana plantation and provides a fascinating insight into how the plant is grown. There are also informative tours of other crops grown on the islands. The small

Puerto de la Cruz is Tenerife's most established resort and caters well for tourists

The parks in Puerto de la Cruz offer welcome shade from the sun

The Virgin Parade, in Puerto de la Cruz, is held on the day of the Immaculate Conception

after about 1½ km (1 mile) you reach another entrance to Puerto. By turning down and following the signs you can reach the resort either above the port or continue on to the lidos.

La Vera is another small village along the way, and is where much of the support industry for the resort is found. About ½ km (¼ mile) further on, amid a mixture of agriculture and industry, is the first turning to Los Realejos which can be seen above the road. The third and final entrance to Puerto is 2km (1 mile) further on, almost opposite the main entrance to Los Realejos. From the road the villages and towns can be seen in the rising hills and beyond the sheer sides of the mountain, along which the inland road twists, in keeping with the gradients. The road runs inland, trapped between often sheer cliffs and the rolling countryside that leads to the now inaccessible coast. Small tunnels protect the road from rock falls while in places the road cuts through the hills. After one of the tunnels you will see the sign to San Vicente. Two kilometres further on is the hidden beach at Playa de Socorro. The beach is approached by a turning off the road to your right and dropping down. This pleasing beach is often busy in the summer, particularly at weekends. Nevertheless it can provide an ideal place for a mid-journey dip. As you emerge from one tunnel, 2km (1 mile) beyond the Los Realejos turning, keep an eye open for the lay-by and *mirador*. From here Puerto and the black rock of the craggy coast can be admired. As you follow the road the coast falls away, 5½ km (3½ miles) after the *mirador* is the town of **San Juan de la Rambla**.

Leaving the *autopista*, you can head inland to La Guancha or by turning down to the coast you descend to Las Aguas, through narrow avenues and lanes lined with trees and flowers. On a calm day you can walk along the rocky coast and swim in the low surf. If the weather is rough then it is best just to sit on the wall and admire the duel between sea and shore.

Back on the main road the route passes through the quiet villages of Santa Catalina and Santo Domingo. There is now a new tunnel that bypasses the village. If it is time to eat or have a well earned break you can enter the village of Santa Domingo either side of the tunnel. Following the tunnel the road swings towards Icod. Here too the road system has recently changed and with good reason. Icod is one of the busiest towns in Tenerife and is also famous for the Drago Tree. (see page 102.) Access to Icod from the north is via a new junction. Follow the road as it splists and after a few hundred metres there is a signpost indicating the access to Icod and la Guancha. Follow the turning up and over and you rejoin the old road that will lead you into the centre of town. If you are bypassing Icod, heading towards Garachico or Guia de Isora then you continue down, leaving Icod sitting above you, until the next junction. This is to Guia. Again you come off the motorway, follow it up and over the left. This will lead you to a roundabout. Guia is well signposted and after the tunnel you come out on the old road above the Drago. By turning left you enter Icod to appear at the Shell station below the tree. In the latter the surface is pitted and bumpy. As you emerge from the village onto a better surface, the view below is of the rock of Garachico and beyond towards Punto Teno. About 3½ km (2 miles) after Santo Domingo is the junction of the island road with the inland route from Los Realejos and la Guancha. Just beyond here, the road enters Icod.

In the next chapter Icod is explored in greater detail but it is worth noting that the main reason for all this investment in by-passes and new roads is the Drago Tree. It is very fashionable to be seen to be caring for the environment and one must applaud the Tenerife authorities for taking traffic away from the very symbol of the island.

Additional Information

Places of Interest

La Laguna

Museo de la Ciencia
(Science Museum)
Via Lacteo
Open: Tues - Sat 10am-5pm
Sun 10am-8pm
☎ 26 34 54

La Orotava
Casa de los Balcones
An historic house that houses a lace
and linen shop.
Open: daily, Monday to Saturday
8.15am-6.30pm. ☎ 33 06 29

Casa Tafuriaste (Ceramics Museum)
La Luz, near La Orotava.
A restored mansion housing a working pottery and fascinating museum
of ceramics. Open: daily 10am-6pm.
☎ 33 33 96

Los Realejos
El Castillo Parque
(Castle Park Museum)
On Puerto-Icod Road
Here the Canary Islands are
explained to the visitor; from flora
and fauna to the volcanoes, culture,
food and agriculture.
Open: daily 9am-6pm.

Puerto de la Cruz
Botanical Gardens
A world famous tropical paradise of
exotic plants and trees.
Open: daily 9am-6pm.
☎ 38475

Casa Iriate
Junction Calle Iriate and Calle San
Juan. This eighteenth-century house
is the birthplace of the author
Tomás Iriate in 1750. Today it is an
artisan centre selling handicrafts.
Above is the Naval Museum which
has a number of excellent models
and dioramas. A small but impressive collection of posters and

paintings are also exhibited here.
Open: daily (hours vary).

Casa de la Real Aduana
(The Royal Customs House)
Calle Las Lonjas
The oldest surviving building in
Puerto, the former customs house is
now a private residence. Built in
1620, the building has been lovingly
restored. The ground floor is open
to the public and around the quite
exquisite patio are a number of old
photographs and artifacts.

Loro Parque and Dolphinarium
A splendid park housing some
1,400 parrots and a dolphinarium.
Live shows and gardens to enjoy.
Open: daily from 8.30am-4pm.
☎ 38 30 12 or 38 30 90

Rose Gardens
There are reputed to be over 10,000
roses in this horticultural paradise.
There are lagoons, bird life and
walks through the array of colour.
Open: daily 9am-5pm.
Free bus from opposite Cafe
Columbus.

Zoolandia
On the northern *autopista*, east of
Puerto de la Cruz. Great fun for the
children, chimp shows and pony
rides, in addition an interesting and
well-kept zoo with many animals to
see. Open: daily from 9am-6pm.
☎ 33 35 09

Tacoronte
El Peñon Golf Course
☎ 63 66 07
Fax: 63 64 80

Tourist Information Centre

Puerto de la Cruz
Plaza de la Iglesia
Open: Monday to Friday 9am-7pm,
Saturday 10am-12noon.
☎ 38 60 00

5

WESTERN TENERIFE

T he western end of the island is a showcase of mountain ranges, coastal plains and lava flows. Behind the cliffs that give Los Gigantes its name is a range of valleys and mountains whose beauty is bewildering. On the coast the lava has flowed to the sea and left an exquisite shoreline. Small villages lie in the lush valleys where the inhabitants remain untouched by the advance of tourism. Each day they toil on the land, often using livestock to pull the plough. Occasionally you come across places like Garachico where the tourists are openly invited to enjoy the facilities available, including taking part in the monthly craft fair.

There are few beaches in the west and they are often inaccessible. Nevertheless, there are areas that are good for swimming and the lava has provided sheltered places where the rocks gracefully meet the sea; the constant battle between the two adds to the spectacle.

This chapter returns to our starting point in Playa de las Americas, so from Icod de los Vinos the route will continue west and then south to Las Americas. In between there is an immense area of natural beauty, both inland and on the coast. There are small villages, beaches, mountains, valleys and a rugged coastline that are all waiting to be discovered.

Icod is one of the most important towns on the island and is a tourist attraction in its own right. Close to the main island road is El Drago (Dragon Tree), which is reputed to be over 3,000 years old. The tree is supported by concrete and steel rods, which cosmetically do little to its grandeur. The Dragon Tree is indigenous to the islands and there are several old examples in Tenerife. When cut, the tree bleeds a red sap, or 'dragon's blood', hence the name. Legend tells of how the Guanche kings held court beneath the canopy. El Drago is

WESTERN TENERIFE

famous throughout the world, and is as much a symbol of the island as Teide.

As noted in the last chapter the road system around Icod and the access to the town has changed to protect the Drago and reduce traffic flow in the busy town. The access from the north is via the new bypass. From Guia you enter Icod by turning right at the roundabout after the tunnel.

Icod has an excellent shopping centre that attracts Canarians from far and wide. The cobbled main street has a wide selection of shops and prices are very reasonable. The town is also one of the oldest inhabited sites on the island. The balconies on the houses near El Drago date from the sixteenth century, simple but attractive wooden structures on the whitewashed houses. Behind El Drago is a large and shady square. On Sundays, as the women go to church, the men sit in the shade provided by the laurel trees. The older part of Icod is well worth exploring. The road that leads up opposite the hotel and between the square and tree is an ideal place to park. Walk up the hill and you come to a small ornate garden around which charming houses have been built. To the left of the garden is the road to town. Continue upwards and you can walk down the narrow streets, another dragon tree can be seen in the garden of one house — it is a younger but impressive example. The church of San Marcos dates from the sixteenth and seventeenth centuries. It is a mixture of Renaissance and Baroque styles and its treasures include a filigree silver cross from Mexico. The convents of San Francisco and San Augustin are also worth visiting, both have fine seventeenth-century carvings.

Having approached Icod from the east along the main island road from Puerto de la Cruz, the route divides into three. Two routes will take you inland along very different routes before coming together at Erjos. The coastal route follows the shoreline to Buenavista before swinging inland through the mountains and then joining the inland road at Santiago del Teide. Such is the variety of scenery, vegetation, sights and sounds that you could quite easily spend several days exploring this area. From Santiago del Teide the main island road continues to Tamaimo. Here the road splits again, providing a coastal route or inland way to Adeje. From Adeje the road leads to Las Americas.

Inland to Erjos

If you are travelling to or from Icod at the end of a long day then the route that cuts out the main road is not only shorter but is peaceful and has much to see along the way. As you leave the centre of Icod heading towards Santa Barbara, turn left at the junction signposted El Amparo. Although you soon leave Icod, the influence of the town remains, for houses, restaurants and service industry line the route as you climb. After about 2km (1 mile) there is a left turn opposite the Los Corales bar. The narrow road climbs rapidly into the hills. Along the way the view across the valley opens out on one side. Just beyond the school, take the left fork and climb still further.

In **Redondo** the villagers are farmers, their *fincas* well tended and productive. The rich soil is ideal for root crops and potatoes are grown in abundance. The strange, cabbage-like plants are not cultivated for human consumption, it seems rabbits prefer this plant to the potatoes and, provided the farmers skirt their land with these, the rabbits will leave the valuable crops alone. The road continues beyond the restaurant for a few kilometres before becoming a track that leads into the pines. This track is a difficult surface at times and is not recommended for ordinary cars.

El Amparo spreads either side of the road from Icod; it is a village which seems to have as many restaurants as houses. The road climbs, providing excellent panoramic views across the Icod valley, before reaching another junction just over 2km (1 mile) beyond the Redondo turning. The dragon tree is visible next to the road that threads its way through the town below. The verdant carpet of bananas on the headland spreads out to sea, with those closest to the sea protected from the salt by plastic houses. Beyond El Amparo you can turn left and inland, by heading straight down you rejoin the main road 2km (1 mile) to the west of Icod.

The inland route takes you along a natural terrace, where to one side are pine forests, and to the other are lava fields and agricultural land which supports the villages. Just after you settle on the route you enter the village of **La Vega**. The streets are narrow and spread out from an equally compressed main street. La Vega is surprisingly large, and has a spacious church. The town is spread out between and beyond the two roads and also up into the hills. Neat houses open directly onto the road and you may well find yourself giving way to pedestrians and livestock as well as cars.

About 2½km (1½ miles) beyond La Vega is a turning on the right that will lead back to the main road at **San Juan de Reparo**. Here you can enjoy another spectacular view; across the valley to the bay that shelters Puerto de la Cruz, and beyond to the far north-eastern headlands. As you enter San Juan head down, follow the streets and

Icod de los Vinos, where the favourable climate produces lush crops

Icod's famous Dragon Tree is reputed to be 3,000 years old

The town of Icod stretches from the coast up into the hillside

The plaza at El Amparo

eventually you will arive at the main road.

About 1km (½ mile) beyond the turning to San Juan the pretty village of **San Francisco de la Montañeta** lies amongst the pines. San Francisco is one of the most attractive villages in Tenerife. The rows of neat houses fall away from the road, sharply contrasting with some of the more untidy villages, the architecture is pleasing to the eye. Note the shrine-like *ermita*. There are a number of these small chapels to be seen around Tenerife. Some are little more than box-like structures. They are sometimes open at one end, flowers and church ornaments can be seen inside. In many secluded villages these *ermitas* serve an important religious purpose and should be respected accordingly.

There is a restaurant at the entrance of the village and from the terrace you can watch the villagers at work in the small plots that adjoin many of the houses. Life seems pleasant here, where the pace of work is dictated by the weather. On Sundays and fiestas (bank holidays) many of the villagers travel the short distance to Arenas Negras. This *zona recreativa* (recreation area) is reached by a track on the left, 700m (760yd) beyond San Francisco. The track enters the forest and climbs to a large open area, one of the largest of these man-made recreation sites. It has barbecues and water supplies as well as an adventure playground for children and a water mine. Access to the gallery is prohibited and there is little to see through the grille barring the entrance, because the 'railway' track leads into the dark interior. If you are lucky enough to visit on a day when the mine is being serviced, it is interesting to see how the water is extracted.

The pines that have become so familiar are less in evidence beyond Arenas Negras. In the 2½ km (1½ miles) before the turning to El Tanque, the left of the road is dominated by lava, spewed and blown from the eruptions in the hills and covered in lichen giving it a ghostly look. The road to El Tanque drops quickly through the *fincas* to emerge onto the main road running parallel below. Continuing for a few hundred metres brings you to the village of **San Jose de los Llaños**. Beyond the small hamlet the road lies open to the left across rich red soil where the villagers grow their crops. The ruins of a church lie just off the road and the Ermita de San Jose can be found here. To the right the land climbs away into the hills. There is an access road by the side of the big fir tree but it is restricted to all terrain vehicles. This is a great shame as only a few kilometres into the interior the network of tracks and firebreaks link and cross the mountains and lava fields. Leaving San Jose behind, the road continues to rejoin the main island road near Erjos.

The Main Island Road:
Icod to Santiago del Teide

The *autopistas* are designed for speed and not sightseeing. From Puerto de la Cruz to Icod the road is straight and of good quality; beyond Icod it climbs, twists, turns and descends until eventually you are back in Las Americas and the *autopista*.

Having entered Icod from the west if your route is planned so that you wish to take the inland road to Santiago del Teide you should follow the road that heads towards the exit for Puerto de la Cruz and look for the junction by the taxi rank. If you turn sharp right, you enter the town centre, by turning right and up the hill you leave the main town centre. The road to El Amparo is signposted at the staggered crossroads.

The access to the main road to Santiago del Teide is best described from the roundabout where all roads meet at the western end of Icod. From the town centre you drop down, past the Shell station and turn left, following the signs to Guia de Isora. As noted previously the Drago will appear on your left and below.

About 2½km (1½ miles) from El Drago there is a junction that will lead you up to the village of La Vega and the inland route described in the previous section. The village of **Genoves** is approached ½km (¼ mile) later. Like many of the towns and villages on the main island road, Genoves has an air of wealth; the church is large and the plaza well cared for.

The twisting road climbs through the verdant countryside; Icod is officially called Icod de los Vinos and it is well-named for the vines are ever present. Beyond Genoves is a wine press, preserved in a small park area. This large machine was often donkey powered, the beast being attached to the upright by a yoke. As the upright screw is revolved the press tightens and the grape juice runs into a reservoir below.

There are a number of lay-bys from where the view to the coast can be enjoyed. Beyond San Juan del Reparo is the Mirador de Garachico, where a large restaurant and souvenir shop have been built. Below, down an almost sheer drop, the coastal village of Garachico can be seen. A solitary rock in the sea is evidence of a violent eruption that all but destroyed the town in 1707. Just beyond the *mirador* is a junction that leads down to the coast and a route that is described in the following section which covers the coastal route.

El Tanque is a busy town, providing banks, post office and the town council for many of the surrounding villages. Just 8½km (5 miles) along the road is a turning to Tierra del Trigo. The road, except for all-terrain vehicles, is a dead end. Nevertheless, it is a pleasing trip down and one that affords excellent views of the northern coast beyond Puerto de la Cruz. You will also come across a mysterious tower, the reasons why it is situated here and seemingly unfinished are unknown.

The road continues to climb through the green agricultural land, which is punctuated by villages. Crops vary for the soil is rich and capable of supporting many varieties; bananas appear next to potatoes, while oranges, vines and avocado can all be seen en route. After nearly 10km (6 miles) a rural track leads inland for 3km (2 miles), joining the inland road west of San Jose.Teide appears soon after and can be seen for the rest of the route. After 13km (8 miles) a wide avenue leads through the pretty village of Ruigomez.

The mountains that dominate the western tip of Tenerife are now in view, rising from the rich plains at the roadside. As you near Erjos, the tops of the nearer mountains may be obscured by mist and this can even happen in summer. The Mountains of Water (Montañas de Agua) are well named as, on entering the tracks and walkways, you find a damp and at times very wet landscape. Deciduous trees grow on the slopes strewn with decaying foliage, under the shaded canopies of the trees. The road climbs steeply into Erjos after 15km (9 miles), where evidence of fire damage can be seen in the gorse — a reminder that fire remains a hazard in many parts of the island. After 17km (10½ miles) the route joins the road from El Amparo.

The inland roads, now joined, continue south westwards. Puerto (door) of Erjos at 1,117m (3,664ft) is well named; as the road climbs up take note of the green scenery, which alters abruptly once you pass through the narrow cutting. The road descends along a twisting ledge providing views into the valley below. The patterns of the *fincas* are easily discerned and, in the valley head, the small hamlet of Valle de Arribal can be picked out.

It is well to remember that this road is the main round island route. Lorries and coaches are commonplace and corners are often blind so you are advised to take great care. The road levels onto the valley floor.

Santiago del Teide is a large village that boasts a number of old and distinguished properties. One that is particularly noteworthy is the building near the church, opposite the small park, with a number of old wine presses in the grounds.

The rugged landscape in the interior of the island

Santiago del Teide from the road to Masca

Along the Coast: Icod to Santiago del Teide

From the roundabout at the western end of Icod follow the signs to Buenavista. You can also continue on the bypass, if coming from Puerto de la Cruz. The two roads join and then drop down onto the coastal plains.

The coastal view opens up and after about ½km (¼ mile) there is an opportunity to leave the main road and head down to the coastal village of **San Marcos.** This resort has grown in stature and is gaining popularity with those seeking smaller and less crowded places. The route down is steep but the surface is good and there is ample room for two cars to pass safely. After 2km (1 mile) there is a car park on the left and from here there is a well-trodden path to the sea. You can park down on the front but there tend to be few spaces. San Marcos remains a small resort with a quiet, secluded beach and safe bathing. Fishing boats add a colourful, traditional feel to the resort, and the bars and restaurants have resisted the temptation of loud, blaring music and neon. Local people visit at the weekends and during fiestas, which is always a good sign.

Beyond the turning to San Marcos the road descends further. It skirts the hills and large numbers of bananas can be seen. Below the road, acres of this valuable crop spread down to the coast in a verdant carpet. The wealth bananas bring is suggested by the fine, colonial-style houses that stand out white amidst the green of the plantations. As the road nears the coast and before Garachico the road is protected from falling rocks by a tunnel twisting down for 700m (760yd) and open to the seaward side so the view can be glimpsed through the circular openings.

Garachico is a large coastal village that has a significant history. The Spanish made the natural harbour one of the most important places in the island. However, in 1707 the volcano above the town erupted and destroyed much of the port below, and the lava that was deposited in the harbour led to a decline in its importance. Today the port supports only a small fleet of fishing boats. One building that survived the volcanic eruption is the church of Santa Ana. This was founded in 1548 and contains some sculptures by Lujón Perez.

As you enter the town the road runs along the promenade. There is a swimming pool alongside the road and Garachico also offers a superb complex of natural pools. These were formed by the lava cooling in contact with the sea, they are fed and cleaned by the tidal action. Between them are paved walkways and there are steps into many of the deeper ones. When the sea is rough, swimming is prohibited, though it can be quite a spectacular sight as the sea crashes and sprays in plumes of white across the offshore lava and the pools. The large pool is open to the sea and, from the small bridge, you can watch the tidal bore that rips along the narrow waterway.

The Castle of San Miguel, behind the pools, houses displays of rocks, shells and artifacts from the island inside its ancient walls. The castle dates from the sixteenth century and its ramparts provide a viewing point across the village and out to the famous rock. The latter has a cross on top of it which represents the prayers of the townspeople that they be spared another catastrophe. The Garachico Craft Fair is held on the first Sunday of each month. There is a handicrafts bazaar with local crafts and produce for sale.

Beyond Garachico the road splits. Past the harbour and quay, from where you can admire the village, the road inland is signposted Las Cruces. Continuing on the coastal road, you climb past the small beach and around the headland; as it straightens out and goes through the banana plantation there is an unsignposted road, just before the right hand bend. It is easily spotted by looking out for the international stop sign on the left. This narrow road leads up into Las Cruces and onto the road that climbs for 7km (4½ miles) to emerge onto the main round island at the Mirador del Garachico. The road is visible below and easily identified by the white blocks that form the safety barrier. As the road climbs out of Garachico the views open to the east and west, offering views across to Buenavista and La Caleta as well as offering an almost aerial view of Garachico.

As the coastal road continues towards Buenavista, on the inland side are the sheer cliffs that form the northern edge of the Montañas de Agua. In winter and spring the water that has fallen as rain can be seen tumbling the height of these cliffs in a foaming waterfall. Just under 1½km (1 mile) after the turning to Las Cruces, the road enters the outskirts of the coastal village of **La Caleta de Interain**. *Caleta* means cove or inlet so it is not surprising to find so many places in Tenerife with this in their name. Although the full names are often longer, the locals will always refer to them by the short, familiar name of La Caleta. There are a number of entrances to the village, and most are signposted. The maze of narrow streets can be confusing.

If you wish to spend time down in the cove, there is a small beach and port, which are easier to enter from Los Silos. The coastline is rocky here but there are some secluded patches of sand. A few kilometres after La Caleta, the straight road enters **Los Silos** which is one of the prettiest villages in Tenerife. Built on the coastal plain in the shadow of the mountains, the village is a busy agricultural centre, around which the *fincas* stretch to the cliff face and to the sea. You are

(Opposite) A panoramic view of the coastal town of Garachico

now entering some of the most fertile land on Tenerife where most crops can be grown with ease. Bananas are plentiful on the coast and can often be seen close to the road, protected by strange blue bags. These bags protect the crop but you will notice they have a light and dark side; by turning one or other side to the sun the farmers can bring on or slow down the ripening process. This allows the labour intensive picking to be carried out on all the trees in one plot together.

Los Silos retains a colonial feel with the painted houses and cobbled main street. In the plaza are a number of pavement bars where you can join the locals in their well earned refreshment. On local fiestas you may find a band playing in the small bandstand in the plaza but the structure is more likely to be hosting the games of local children.

As you leave Los Silos there is a turning on the coastal side signposted El Puertito. By following the road down and along the newly constructed route you reach modern bungalows and apartments that have been built on the sea's edge. There is an excellent swimming pool here which is popular with the Canarians but rarely crowded. By following the route to the side of the apartments and along the dirt track towards the deserted factory with the chimney, you pass a small beach and enter almost opposite the beach of La Caleta. Los Silos and the villages that make up this north-western coast have, to some extent, avoided tourism's advance. Remote and reached by long, winding routes, only recently have they been seen as potential sites for development. However, for now, they retain their beauty and tranquillity.

Buenavista is the largest settlement in this part of Tenerife. It, too, relies on agriculture rather than tourism but offers the visitor plenty to see and do. As you enter the town from Los Silos, look for the Firestone sign and by turning left you reach the road to Santiago del Teide. If you miss it do not worry, as the main turning is only a few hundred metres later. Buenavista receives many visitors because it lies on the junction of the roads running along the coast and across the mountain range behind the town. However, the town is much more than a junction so, before heading inland to Santiago, you may wish to take advantage of the shops, banks and commercial facilities that Buenavista has. There are also a number of routes you can explore beyond the town.

Bypassing the turning to Palmar, turn left at the staggered cross-roads, where you may notice the faded sign indicating that this road leads to Teno. Stay on the road and soon on your right is a signpost to the beach (*playa*). The beach at the end provides some sand, rocks and rock pools. By parking and exploring on foot you will find your own spot along the quiet coast.

By continuing along the surfaced road you climb quickly along a road cut into the side of the cliff. Below the coast is rugged, foaming white as the surf hits the submerged lava offshore. Banana plantations stretch down to the shore, cottages and houses gleam white in the sun. Under the arch is a viewing point, revealing a small cove which lies hemmed in by giant lava cliffs. The surf crashes against the beach and rocks below, creating rainbows as the sun hits the spray, the colour adding life to the glistening rock. It is certainly a spectacular scene when the sea is rough.

The track continues to climb, its surface much improved and with work still being carried out. Barriers have been built alongside the track as it climbs. The reason for the track will not be apparent yet and the work that has been devoted to the route is puzzling. Soon after the arch you enter the first of two tunnels which have been cut square into the rock face. There is no lighting so headlights are essential. Dust hangs in the air and the interior has a decidedly eerie atmosphere. You emerge into sunlight briefly before entering the second, longer tunnel. Once back into daylight, the track drops to run almost straight to Punta Teno. The mountains rise inland and you drive along the edge of the coastal plain, the plain below runs to the coast. The land is farmed in places and there is a large house that stands alone. From above the plain one can see the coast and the bays eroded by the sea although access is not allowed as the land is private. About 5km (3 miles) from the tunnel you reach the end of the track.

❊ **Punta Teno** is the most westerly point on Tenerife. Two lighthouses have been constructed here. Although they are not open to the public, you are free to wander around the site. You can also stand on the point, beyond the buildings, and look out over the sea to La Palma and Gomera, back along the coast of Tenerife to Buenavista and to Los Gigantes. It is hoped that a maritime museum will be opened in the older lighthouse, thereby preserving the building and providing an interesting diversion. There is a small, safe beach and after a dip in the cool, azure waters one can explore the spits of lava and the headland. Fishing boats are kept in houses hewn from the rock and are launched down primitive slipways. By looking south on a clear day you can see the buildings of Los Gigantes to the south and in the foreground are the sheer cliffs from which the resort takes its name.

The Inland Route from Buenavista to Santiago del Teide

The inland route from Buenavista to Santiago del Teide is one of the more spectacular, scenic and interesting roads in Tenerife. It crosses a high mountain range, skirts deep gorges and travels through villages where little has changed for many years, with a few concessions to the tourist traffic. The road has been improved and made safer — what was once a dirt track used by donkeys and mules is now tarmaced and protected by barriers. As you leave Buenavista the climb, which is gentle at first, takes you through well-tended *fincas* of rich brown soil. Mountain spurs fall to the valley floor and terracing climbs upwards. The rustic dwellings seem deserted and indeed many are; no longer homes, they are used as stores and for animals.

The town of **El Palmar** lies in the valley amid lush *fincas* and the green of this agricultural land. The road cuts to the western side of the town, but as you run alongside the houses keep an eye open for the original village. A collection of stonewalled houses sit at the edge of the land farmed by the same families for centuries. Times are changing here, for there are newer houses and a number of restaurants along the road. Nevertheless, El Palmar retains the atmosphere of a sleepy town that relies on hard work and the richness of the soil to provide the inhabitants with a livelihood.

Just beyond El Palmar is the strange sight of a hill cut away as if it were a cake. The wedge-shaped cuts are not natural; the lava and soil below the surface have been mined for breeze blocks and other building materials. From close up, the scars detract from the beauty of the hill but later, as you climb, the view over the mound adds character to the landscape.

The road continues to climb revealing a patchwork of *fincas* and fields in a mixture of green and gold. After about 8½km (5½ miles) you skirt the tiny hamlet of Las Lagunatas and, soon after, you can turn off the road to enter El Monte de Agua. The road soon becomes rough and potted as it rises over the mountains and descends to emerge in Erjos. The views from the heights are spectacular but even in summer the route is only passable in all terrain or high vehicles. In winter the water from the hills and mountains leaves the valley track wet, muddy and difficult to negotiate in anything other than four wheel drive cars and jeeps.

Beyond Las Lagunatas the road starts to climb in earnest, the route following the side of the mountain before becoming a road cut into the cliff face. You leave the green of the roadside to climb above the valley and to look back across the floor of this farming community. The terraces can be seen climbing between the sheer, talon-like rock spurs providing shade and a source of moisture for the *fincas*.

After 12km (7½ miles), having climbed to the top of the mountain, you reach La Cumbre (the summit). Here the road crosses the peak and the valley opens up below on either side. The two valleys are very different. To the north is the valley of El Palmar and fertile terraced land; to the west are gorges and rocky ravines of volcanic rock where little grows on the steep sides. If you stop at the lay-by and look down into the valley, some interesting characteristics of the volcanic heritage of the island can be seen. The rocks which form a wall that divides the barren land are dykes, streams of lava that cooled in the cracks and fissures of the rock when molten. Lava remains less prone to erosion than the surrounding rock which, as it erodes, leaves the lava as a dividing wall.

The road now heads down into the valley of **Las Carrizales**. This hamlet is at the top of a deep gorge in which the land is farmed. The work that generations of families have done must be seen to be really appreciated. From the lava and rock, terraces have been hewn and then walled. Tracks have been cut into the valley side and then soil toiled for crops. The village lies below the road, a small settlement gathered around a small church. For the next few kilometres the gradient is gentler as you climb to the next peak. After about 15km (9 miles) you cross La Cumbre to view the Masca valley below. The view is breathtaking, and opposite are the sheer cliffs that tower over the valley below, presenting weathered faces of varying strata and unbelievable beauty. Then the route twists down until you enter the village of Masca.

The history of **Masca** is subject to so much legend that one finds the truth and fiction interwoven. The birth of the village is something of a mystery. Set away from the road, inland and in a valley that remains relatively unexplored, it is hard to imagine who wanted to live here and how they found it in the first place. One of the most plausible stories is that a fisherman, marooned on the beach at the foot of the valley, walked inland and found the rich valley where Masca now stands. Finding rich soil, ample water and a somewhat idyllic paradise, he went home, collected his family and founded Masca.

This sleepy, beautiful hamlet, situated in a valley of immense beauty, is one of Tenerife's most visited spots. No longer off the beaten track, Masca attracts many visitors daily. As the road de-

A winding road leads down the Masca valley

scends into the village, past waterfalls and palm trees, it seems a tranquil, untouched place and to some extent remains an unspoilt beauty spot. From the road you can walk down and explore the narrow streets, admire the rustic architecture and sample one of the excellent restaurants.

The road skirts the top of the village before climbing again. It can be identified by the pink block barriers, as it snakes skywards. For about 3½km (2½ miles) it ascends towards yet another *cumbre*. There is an auto-bar here, so by parking in the lay-by you can take refreshment and look back over the valley and beyond to Gomera and La Palma. By walking down to the previous bend you can view the road as it meanders to Masca and the village itself in the valley floor. Teide can now be seen again, rising above the foothills. The black scars of lava above Santiago del Teide, on the Arguayo road, are obvious against the burnt yellow of the surrounding agricultural land. The road from here quickly descends into Santiago del Teide.

Santiago del Teide lies at the head of the valley that runs down to the coast, and at the foot of the valley that leads inland. Being on the main round island road, the town has some importance and governs most of the western part of Tenerife including Los Gigantes.

From Santiago del Teide there are two routes, both of which meet at Chio but not before the lower road has divided, enabling the western coast to be reached above Los Gigantes. The coastal and inland routes then head towards Adeje where they join again and head to Playa de las Americas.

Between the routes are country lanes that criss-cross farmland and *barrancos*. You can therefore head off along one route and then change to the other. After leaving Santiago del Teide, the road to Arguayo and to Chio is found on the left, and this scenic route is well worth exploring if you intend to head on the inland route to the resorts of the south.

After passing through the tiny hamlet of Las Manchas, the road climbs above the valley and through the almond orchards to Arguayo. There is much to see on the short distance the route covers; above Las Manchas the views are of the Santiago valley and across to the hills above Masca. As the road descends it crosses the barren scars of lava which spread down the hills, between which terraces have been built. **Arguayo** is a small industrious village where narrow streets house a population that farm the surrounding land. Here too is a small but interesting artisan centre called the Centro Alfrarero de Arguayo which is a ceramics museum with a working pottery (see the Additional Information section at the end of the chapter for more details). From here the road descends to join the main round island road just west of Chio.

The continuation of the island road from Santiago heads down to Tamaimo through land that has often been left to fallow. Here the employment opportunities of nearby resorts has encouraged many of the young people of these villages to leave. While they may still live in the villages, many do not work here, so the fallow land awaits either sale for development or will be reclaimed by nature.

About 1km (½ mile) after the road to Arguayo, the hamlet of **El Molledo** can be seen. Below the road, houses sit among *fincas* and almond trees. These trees and those on the Arguayo road bloom in the early months of the year, when the land is pink and white with blossom. The road descends further, through the village of El Retamar and down into Tamaimo. Along the way a large valley opens before you where, beyond the settlement of Tamaimo, the coast and the resort of Playa de la Arena can be seen. Above, the valley sides are craggy and steep. After about 4½km (2½ miles) look east and you will see the water canal as it meanders along the cliff face. This vital supply must have been a taxing project for those that built it to bring water to the arid valley floors. After 6km (4 miles) you enter the town of **Tamaimo**.

This bustling settlement earns its importance from the junction of the main road with the road to and from Los Gigantes. Here, in the valley, summers can be very hot and in winter equally cold, but many Canarians have made their homes in Tamaimo. As you admire the surrounding scenery it is not difficult to understand why. On either side of the town are the towering valley sides of weathered cliffs and spurs of varying colour, behind it the valley continues and below are the resorts and the sea. From Tamaimo you can head down to the sea or carry on eastwards along the island road. After 6½km (4 miles) you meet the junction.

The Inland Route

From Tamaimo the road skirts the cliff face and heads towards Chio. This route takes you through the heartland of south-west Tenerife. Here tourism has had a limited impact. The villages retain their unspoilt character and only a few foreigners have settled in this area. However, the winds of change are blowing, for already much of the land is earmarked for possible development. As you climb away from Tamaimo, the views of the valley and cliffs are spectacular, though as the road meanders along the cliff face it is difficult to find

Country house and fincas *below Chio*

*Almond blossom
in the Arguayo
valley*

somewhere to pull over and admire the panorama. The route is narrow and hemmed in by the cliffs and study barriers. By the time the road widens, much of the view has been lost.

After 4km is the junction leading to Arguayo. The road to Teide is to the left of this complicated junction. Caution is a good idea here. The road markings are often obscured by the curve of the road surface. Chio is below the road, a busy village that relies, as all the settlements do here, on income from agriculture. From Chio you can descend to the coast using the rural lanes that weave their way through the *fincas* and plantations. By turning down by the school, left at the end and taking the right fork the road will lead away from Chio.

Chio itself is a village of narrow streets and interesting rustic architecture. The plaza is large and there is a notable steepled church. The village has a number of small shops and banks. Soon after leaving Chio you pass the entrance to Chiguergue and another access route to the mountain. Just before you enter Guia de Isora there is a turning to the coast signposted Playa San Juan. Details of this and the other cross-country routes are given later in this chapter.

Guia de Isora, like Santiago del Teide, is important as a centre of commerce, and the town council for much of the surrounding area is based here. The shopping centre is spread out but comprehensive and is built around the plaza. The church has immense tradition and beauty. Inside an ornate Madonna stands over the stone pillars and pews. Guia is developing quickly, its reliance on agriculture reduced as the coastal resorts which the town governs are developed and their incomes are counted. Nevertheless, it retains the feeling of a market town.

Beyond Guia the island road crosses a shelf between mountain and coastal plain. Below is the sea and resorts that are now being developed. Inland the plantations and *fincas* remain in use and further inland are the rocks, b*arrancos* and mountains of the island's interior. The road goes through two tunnels and through the village of Tejina de Guia. Five kilometres (3 miles) after leaving Guia you reach a junction. Head down and you emerge onto the coastal road east of San Juan, head inland and you will reach the village of **Vera de Erques**.

The road is a dead end but that should not dissuade you from leaving the main road and climbing the 6km (4 miles) to this village. The village itself is small, compact and sits astride a *barranco*. Surrounding the village are *fincas,* perched high above the coast. The newer houses that can be seen on the route enjoy a view across the island to the sea. At night the neon signs of Las Americas create a second sunset and in the distance the lights of Gomera are reflected in the sea. There are a number of bars and restaurants in the village, at which you will receive a friendly welcome. Beyond the village the road continues as a dirt track into the mountains. About half way along the route is a turning that leads into Tejina, although the road surface is crumbling and it is best to return the way you climbed (the road down to the coast is described on page 133).

Two kilometres (1 mile) further down the main road is another turning, this time heading inland to the villages of La Concepción and Tijoco de Arriba. Below the road is the village of Tijoco. These inland hamlets are little more than a few houses around a plaza and church, but are worth a visit if only to look back over the agricultural land to the sea. From here the resorts of Callao Salvaje and Playa Paraíso shine in the shimmering heat of the day. The land here is fertile and actively farmed. Vines border the *fincas* where potatoes and peppers are grown in abundance. The restaurant here is popular, a local eating house of rustic charm where the food is basic but excellent.

Nearly 2km (1 mile) after the church is a small track leading off to the right. At first the track is passable in cars and remains so if you are an experienced driver. For those less confident, carry on for a few hundred metres until the *barranco* opens before you. From here you can look down deep into the gorge and admire the scenery of this dried up river bed. In winter you may see a trickle of melt-water but the bed usually remains dry and arid. Goats can be seen along the path opposite, looking for shade and food on the valley floor. With a high vehicle the road is more negotiable and leads to the village of Taucho.

The turning to Taucho lies 1½km (1 mile) beyond the Tijoco/Concepción junction. It is easily missed as it is a sharp turn and also on a bend, though it is signposted and there are a number of commercial units on the turning itself. The climb is steep but the road has been resurfaced. **Taucho** is one of the most traditional and certainly one of the most attractive villages in Tenerife. By following the road up and through the village you reach the bar/restaurant and beyond that cross the *barranco* into a small hamlet called Los Picos, beyond here the track is either private or impassable. The serene tranquillity of these hamlets is contagious. Although the inhabitants face a journey of 6km (4 miles) to the main road it is not too difficult to understand why they remain here.

Taucho, Vera de Erques and La Concepción are so tranquil and pretty and enjoy such views of the surrounding countryside that one wonders why anyone would want to leave here. Yet the nearby resorts are the centre of attraction both for visitors and the authorities. The waiting lists for telephones stretch to years in the villages, planning permission is expensive and the resorts dictate the prices of materials and labour. Living in these villages can be frustrating and arduous, so perhaps those who stay do so simply because this is where their families have lived for centuries.

The Coastal Route

The road from Tamaimo drops quickly to the coast. The valley sides steepen as the floor widens, and the route twists down until it splits after nearly 6km (4 miles). If you turn along the road to Alcala you can avoid the congestion of the resorts. By continuing down, the entrance to Los Gigantes can be reached 1km (½ mile) down the road.

Los Gigantes is a small, tranquil resort, named after the giant cliffs that rise from the sea. Hemmed in, it has not been able to grow as much as the other southern resorts and this fact, together with the careful consideration given to Los Gigantes by the planners, make the area a select place with much to offer. The road snakes down to the one way system. Just before the marina the road right leads to the beach, and it is often easy to park here. The beach is small but rarely crowded and enjoys a beautiful setting in the shadow of the cliffs. The surf is low and the shore slopes gently to the deeper water so it is ideal for children. Scuba diving is popular here and the water is certainly clear. The marina is full of boats, including those offering trips to fish or to see the dolphins that play offshore. The commercial heart of Los Gigantes is small but offers a variety of quality shops and restaurants. However, the resort is too hilly to be suitable for disabled people. Los Gigantes remains a small resort, but one to which many people return to year after year.

Further around the coast, the small fishing village of **Puerto de Santiago** has retained little of the charm of the small port it used to be. Hotels, villas and apartments now dominate, overlooking the craggy coastline. The harbour remains, however, and you can sit on the quay and watch the fishermen at work. One of the bays has fine, dark sand but the beach shelves quickly so it is a good idea to keep a close eye on children.

Playa de la Arena has an excellent natural beach that is very good for swimming. At the back of the beach are a number of shops and restaurants as well as increasing numbers of apartment blocks. Had

The promenade at Playa de la Arena

Los Gigantes is still a small resort despite the growth of holiday apartments

The dark sand at Playa de la Arena indicates the island's volcanic origin

you visited here less than 10 years ago, only a fraction of the developments could be found but, despite the building, the resort is pleasant, attracting many people who spend time on the beach or dive from the rocks adjoining the beach. The sand is black but this beach is considered to be one of the finest on the island. In rough weather you may see a red flag warning that swimming is dangerous but there are plenty of other things to see and do in the resort. The road continues for about 1km (½ mile) before rejoining the road from Tamaimo to Alcala.

The south-western coast of Tenerife has yet to see the massive development that has taken place in Playa de las Americas, though there are resorts along the coast road where you can stop to enjoy a dip in a pool, lido or the sea. The coast remains virtually unspoilt and has plenty of secluded coves, bays and beaches. After turning off the Tamaimo/Los Gigantes road, you skirt the back of the resorts of Playa de la Arena and Puerto de Santiago. Before you reach the entrance to Playa Arena on the left are a number of local restaurants. This road leads up to the inland web which is described on page 133 Past the entrance to Playa del Arena the road passes an arid area leading to the sea. The desert has tracks across it and there is a small beach and a number of rock pools where local children fish for crabs and octopus.

In the village of **Alcala**, entered 2km (1 mile) after Playa de las Arenas, is a small port where the fishermen tend their boats and nets on the quay. Alcala is expanding and the banana plantations are earmarked for further development, but it is still a delightful village with a good shopping centre and a large tree-lined plaza where fiestas are often held. At these, you can join the locals dancing into the early hours.

Playa de San Juan, like Alcala, has seen much development in recent years. The port has been expanded and the village is now spreading westwards as the plantations on the coast are flattened and apartments and villas spring up in their place. The fishing boats that sway at anchor in the port provide the restaurants of San Juan with fresh fish daily. The beach is small and has little sand but the sea is clean and swimmers are able to dive from the port and rocks in safety. San Juan is earmarked for further development, though the signs are that this expansion will be carefully planned so that the resort will not be spoiled for future visitors. Just beyond San Juan is a road leading to Guia de Isora.

East of San Juan the road runs almost parallel to the coast. The region is arid and the soil for the plantations is often imported.

Bananas and tomatoes are the principal crops here, protected from the winds by walls and from the sun by plastic housing. *Fincas* spread inland and up into the hills, though the gradient inland is shallow. Above the plantations the white dots of villages further inland can be seen. Behind them is Teide, the light coloured ravines visible on its slopes in good weather.

The road winds for 8km (5 miles) until, on a straight, there is a turning that leads to the round island route below Vera De Erques, 2½km (1½ miles) beyond is Marazul. Built in the middle of a banana plantation this aparthotel is one of the most luxurious and prestigious complexes on the island and was originally a timeshare resort. Much of the building is now owned privately and high prices are sought for the privilege of living in such luxury.

Two and half kilometres (1½ miles) further down the coast is **Callao Salvaje**. Development continues here and while the bars, restaurants and sporting facilities are open to the general public, the pools are private and entrance is restricted.

Playa Paraíso, which is 1km (½ mile) further on, does have an ❋ excellent lido which is open to the public. There is an entrance charge but once inside there is an excellent pool and a small beach in a rocky cove. Volleyball is often organised for the energetic visitor who is not content to lie by the pool and there are also one or two restaurants in the resort. Playa Paraíso has yet to be finished and although construction has been continuing for many years, it remains a small resort.

Beyond Playa Paraíso and just after leaving the village of Armeñime, there is a turning signposted El Puertito. The new tarmac road is worth following down to the sea. After 600m (650yd) the road forks. Take the right fork and the track heads down for just over 3km (2 miles). **El Puertito** is a strange place, nestling in a small bay, and can only be approached by the track or from the sea. You first catch sight of the village through the deserted plantations as you emerge above the bay where fishing boats can be seen.

The bay is earmarked for future development, up until recently a number of houses on stilts and beach houses constructed by locals adorned its sides. Following the council's decision these were unceremoniously demolished and, although the bar remains, El Puertito lost some of its character. On the shore itself is a small sandy beach and a bar where you can join the fishermen as they discuss the day's catch. El Puertito is one of the most serene and delightful places on Tenerife and yet it lies only a few miles along the coast from Las Americas. Perhaps the locals are keeping the port a secret, for it

Fishing boats in the harbour, Playa de san Juan

(Opposite) Pirate ship cruise, Playa de san Juan

The church at Playa de san Juan

remains untouched and unspoilt.

At the fork, just off the road, take the left fork and then opposite the house turn right down the side of the plantation. This track leads down to one of the most beautiful, unspoilt beaches in the Canary Islands. After about 1½km (1 mile) follow the road to the left. By heading straight on you will reach the top of the cliffs to the east of El Puertito. By now the track is difficult in all but a jeep, so it is best to park and follow the track to the wooden bridge. Cross this handbuilt but sturdy structure and walk the well-worn track to the house. Climb the steps behind the house and continue along the path. After about ½km (¼ mile) the beach is visible in front of you. The sand is 'yellow' and the surf is ideal for swimming. This beach is home for a small community of naturists, though you can stretch out on the beach and enjoy the sun without feeling obliged to strip off. Along the far end of the beach, and around the headland, is another beach, where a number of people live in tents and shacks. Again recent proposals for development have seen a few of the shacks demolished. There are no facilities here at all so take food and drink. The clifftop walk leads to La Caleta and as the road continues to the junction below Adeje, La Caleta can also be approached by road. About 1km (½ mile) beyond the turning to El Puertito, the coastal road rejoins the main round island route, just south of Adeje.

The Inland Web

Before returning to Las Americas, it is worth exploring the tangled web of roads and tracks that join the inland road and coastal route. From just east of Los Gigantes to beyond Playa San Juan on the coast and between Chio and Vera de Erques inland, are a number of access points to the heart of the coastal plains and the hills that rise from the coast. These roads are narrow but have good surfaces, and they are easy to navigate providing you are in no hurry. Today the roads are tarmaced, though they were built originally as dust tracks giving access to the many *fincas* and plantations and were, until recently, little more than cinder lanes. There remain some that cannot be negotiated by car. Navigating these roads is simple; go up and you will meet the main island road, go down and you meet the coastal road.

The routes are best taken at a leisurely pace, so that the views of villages, hills and Teide can be appreciated. From the viewpoints high up in the region, the coastal plain seems so far away. You climb quickly and soon the fishing ports of Alcala and San Juan can be seen almost in plan view. Surf and white horses dance and crash against the rocky coast, which remains largely untouched by tourism. The plantations finish abruptly just inland and in the centre of the region is a defined area where the land has been left fallow. Occasionally a villa can be admired but the land remains hot and arid, often devoid of life except for hardy cacti and grasses.

Higher up, the land is cultivated and the co-operatives at Guia and Tejina are busy with the produce of the surrounding landowners. Tomatoes, marrows, potatoes and peppers are the main crops, and farmers' lorries and jeeps can often be seen climbing the hills to market. It is hard to tell how long the *fincas* will be able to resist the developers — a complex is already being constructed on the road down from Tejina to the east of San Juan. The desire of residents and tourists alike to escape the bustle of the coast suggests that, in future, this area will see further development. However, for now it remains an unspoilt region, with spectacular views and countryside offering something of interest around every bend.

Back to Las Americas

Adeje is one of the more historic towns in Tenerife which remains a very important settlement. From this quiet, unassuming town much of Las Americas is governed. There are three entrances to this beautiful town. The first is at the junction where the inland road from Guia is joined by the coastal route from San Juan. The second is less than a kilometre further on, turning right at the petrol station will allow you to join the road from the previous junction. Turn right at the end and you soon enter the town. If you turn left at this junction the road twists and turns down to the port of La Caleta.

As the main road continues it widens. As you pass the large Agricultural Co-operative on your right keep an eye out for the signs to Adeje. You leave the main road, sweep up and over and then climb, entering the town just below the main square. There is much to see and do, the traditional church is large and impressive, and there are a number of good shops and eating houses.

Adeje is growing as it responsibilities and importance spread. It does, however, retain a pleasing traditional feel and offers the visitor much to see. Above the town is the famous Barranco de Infierno. For those who are willing to trek along the mountainside for 2 hours the reward at the end is a spectacular waterfall, as well as impressive and extensive views along the way. The entrance to the *barranco* lies at the top of the western part of the town and, by turning right at the old cannon, you reach the car park.

Continue along the island road beyond the crossroads that join this and the coastal routes to reach another crossroads on which a Mobil filling station stands. Turn left and you approach Adeje. Las Americas stands a few kilometres further on, or turn right to head down to the small port and growing resort of **La Caleta**.

The quiet port has seen much development in recent years and this is still continuing. From the road the route to the sea continues down a *barranco* for 3½km (2½ miles), twisting and turning until reaching a T junction. By carrying straight on you head towards the original port. The village roads are unmade but parking and then exploring is the best way to see La Caleta. Steps lead from the lava flows into the sea, while to the west is a small but sandy beach and, further round still, a smooth lava flow providing a firm but comfortable sunbathing spot. The coast and clifftops to the west can be explored and by walking a short distance the beaches to the east of El Puertito can be seen from above.

By turning left at the T junction you enter the newer part of the resort. Villas, apartments and hotels have been built here but the resort remains quiet. After about 2km (1 mile), just past the large church, the road swings inland. As the road climbs a beach is visible. It is accessible by turning down the track. Always quiet, perhaps because of the pebbles, the beach can provide a base for wading into the surf for a cooling dip. The road continues for another 2km (1 mile) before emerging onto the island road, to the west of Las Americas.

Inland from Adeje, the island route continues straight and then descends into Las Americas. The views of Las Americas are impressive, particularly at night. It feels a little strange to be driving through desert knowing that the urban sprawl of the resort is so near. The road passes the few remaining banana plantations before entering Las Americas at Torviscas.

Additional Information

Places of Interest

Arguayo
Centro Alfarero de Arguayo
A ceramics museum and working pottery. Open: Monday to Saturday 10am-1pm and 4-6pm.
☎ 86 31 27

Tourist Information Centre

Playa de la Arena
Avda Maritima
Open: Monday to Friday 9am-6pm, Saturday 10am-1pm.
☎ 11 03 48

6

TEIDE
AND THE NATIONAL PARK

T he interior of the island is a very special place. The peak of Teide stands in vigil over the remains of old volcanoes that have spewed forth rivers of lava that now stand silent in the thin air. Sunken craters leave a spectrum of coloured rock on which only the hardiest of plants can grow. Rocks blown from the mountain still stand today where they fell, silent witnesses to the rage of eruptions. Sheer and craggy sides surround the approaches to the foot of Teide and then there is the peak itself; conical, often snowcapped and always beautiful. The fascinating 'lunar' landscape gives the impression that mother nature created this in one of her angriest but most inspired moments.

Below the National Park are the pine forests. The Canarian pine is a vital part of the ecology of the island, for the island gets its water from the trees. As the clouds descend, so the trees absorb the moisture, releasing the excess into the porous rock. From here it is mined and then runs to the coast in narrow, fast flowing canals.

You cannot but be impressed by Teide, it has a certain majesty that attracts people, so that even regular visitors and residents are drawn back time and time again. Apart from being the highest point in 'Spain', Teide is a symbol of Tenerife and a tangible asset of which the Canarians are justifiably proud. At 3,717m (12,192ft) above sea level, the volcano stands proud above the island, visible from almost all areas of Tenerife and from the more westerly islands. Some claim that on a good day the islands of Lanzarote and Fuerteventura are visible and that beyond them even the coast of Africa can be seen.

This chapter will cover not just Teide but the National Park and the access roads from the coast. You can approach the National Park from four directions, and these roads split again as they head down, so this chapter will include the roads from Chio in the west, Vilaflor in the south, Güimar and La Laguna in the east, and La Orotava in the north.

The National Park and the surrounding countryside can be divided into definite geological and ecological areas, all of which will be described in the text. However, a general picture of the area in question will enable you to plan your routes accordingly. On the south and west routes you climb through pine forests, which peter out at between 1,600 and 1,800m (5,250 and 5,900ft). To the west they are replaced by lava rivers; cold dark rock where little grows. In the south the road winds through the sides of the sunken crater to join the western route at Boca de Tauce.

From the north the pine forests are again in evidence as the route meanders towards the start of the National Park. Along the route there are sharp valleys and sheer escarpments hidden beyond the trees, complimented by impressive views to the coast. The eastern roads join above Arafo. The road from La Laguna follows a ridge along the backbone of the island with views to both the north and south; these are always of interest and often spectacular. The road to Arafo winds up from the agricultural heartland of the south and east of the island. Arafo is famous for its wine and, as the road climbs, vines can be seen clinging to the walls and terraces.

The different routes are very individual, although all provide views across the hills and plains to Teide. Just as the routes differ, so does the view of Teide. Approached from the north with the surrounding foothills hidden, it seems alone and taller. In winter, as the sun sets, the red reflects in the pure white of the snow and the mountain takes on a soft, pink glow. From the east Teide dominates the horizon as if the world ends beyond its peak. From the west and south the view of the mountain is interrupted by foothills and the old peak (*pico viejo*). Only as the road opens onto the plain below the peak, is the first pure view of Teide to be enjoyed.

The National Park of Las Cañandas del Teide covers an area of over 130sq km. Dominated by the peak of Teide, the park is controlled by a government authority and some areas have strict restrictions on access. There are also a number of regulations in force which are listed later on in this chapter. Most of the park is readily accessible to the public, and the roads skirt its southern and western edges before cutting across towards the foot of Teide.

The park is a world apart from the rest of Tenerife. Its special climatic, ecological and geological conditions all directly influence the area's flora and wildlife. At 2,000m (6,500ft) above sea level the changes in climate are dramatic. During the day the sun's heat throws a shimmering haze across the land, whereas in winter and at night the cold descends and it is not unusual to see the plants covered in ice as a new day dawns. What little precipitation there is falls as snow. To stand in the crater, with the sun high in the azure sky, and see a distinct line of snow draped over the peak, is a haunting sight. In times of bad weather the roads can be closed by snow, but any lengthy closure is rare.

The flora that grows in the park is surprisingly abundant, hardy flowers and plants often blossom in spring to add more colour to the existing profusion of shades. Many plants are low, bush-like clumps, spreading across the arid soil in search of moisture. Most common are the yellow, thorny Pajonera and the blue Teide's herb, and most spectacular is the Tajinaste, a striking, rich red plant which grows to a height of over 2m ($6^1/_2$ft). A number of these majestic plants grow close to the road and are easily spotted when in bloom.

The plants have proved more hardy than the wildlife. With little shade from the heat or protection from the cold, many species only live on the lower slopes. Hares are commonplace on the ground, while birds of prey circle above in the thermals, waiting for a lizard or hare to break cover. The lizards (these are harmless) can be seen scurrying between the rocks looking for insects. They are timid creatures and there are a number of varieties, some of which can grow to over 25cm (10in) long. There are many birds in the park; sparrows and robins are often spotted, while the attractive blue chaffinch may be seen showing off its plumage, perched on a bush or rock. Sparrow hawks are common, wheeling close to the cliffs where they nest, and kestrels can be seen stalling and diving as they spot movement below.

The Route from the South

As you head east from Las Americas the first access road is Vilaflor. Once past Vilaflor, the road begins to climb and, as it does so, the pine forests become more dense. The pine forests that surround Teide's foothills are as spectacular as they are resilient. In places the trees cling to a minimum of soil with roots clawing in mid air as the terrain falls away to the road or into a valley. The trees are protected by law and there are very severe penalties for those foolish enough to start fires or damage the trees in any way. You can of course wander at your leisure through the pines which are not as tall as their European cousins but are hardy, surviving extreme conditions. The tempera-

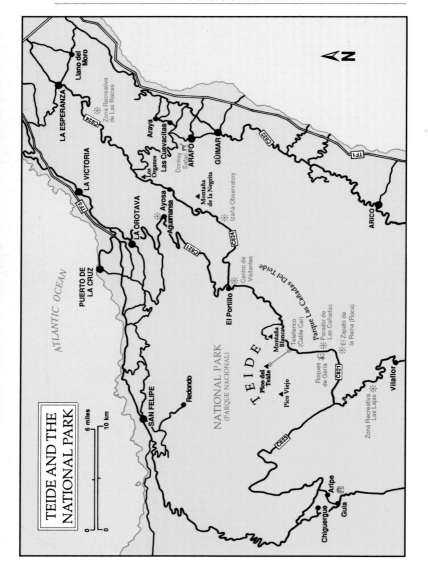

(Opposite) The lunar-like landscape of the Teide National Park

ture variance above 1,500m (4,900ft) is great, it can snow in winter and be hot and dry in summer.

It is surprising just how much of interest lies beyond the roads to Teide. Small tracks lead off the tarmac road, but they are generally only passable in four wheel drive vehicles or lorries. However, their condition will normally allow you to drive a few hundred metres in from the road.

As you climb from Vilaflor there are fine views in every direction. Those to the coast show the built up resorts as little more than faint specks of white below the horizon. The road is of good quality, twisting upwards in tight turns that can leave you almost dizzy. However, it is quite safe, for corners that have sheer or steep drops to the side are protected by barriers.

Vilaflor can be approached from two southerly directions. It is an attractive town that is nestled in a narrow and shallow valley, visible from across the *barranco* as you climb from Granadilla. Vilaflor is an agricultural centre, there are even *fincas* within the town. Past the town entrance is a *mirador* — from high above the town you can look back across the countryside and the town itself. The land stretches to the sea in the distance, individual *fincas* being easily distinguished, particularly those with the whitish pumice.

Vilaflor is a pleasant town and one that provides a welcome break on your travels. Should you decide to bypass Vilaflor, you will find that as you climb to the side of the town, past the *mirador*, the town opens up below you. From here the *fincas* that contrast dramatically with the town's buildings can clearly be seen within its boundaries. Depending on the time of year you visit, these *fincas* are green with crop or in fallow awaiting the next year's produce.

From Vilaflor the drive to Teide is one of the most scenic and certainly one of the most spectacular routes to be found in Tenerife. Beyond the town the climb to above 2,000m (6,500ft) is not as abrupt as you might expect; in fact it takes over 15km (9 miles) to climb a litle over 600m (1,970ft). The shallow gradient does not make the journey any less impressive; in fact, as the road twists with contours, views open up in every direction. After about 20km (12$^1/_2$ miles) a good view of Gran Canaria appears on the horizon. Here, at about 1,220m (4,000ft), the pines are thin on the ground — the *barrancos* and the gradient of the slopes away from the road make it difficult for this most hardy of trees to grow in the numbers found on the north of the island.

After about 25km (15$^1/_2$ miles) you can break your journey at another *zona recreativa*, **Las Lajas**. For many, this is journey's end as they set about cooking over a wood-fired barbecue, tasting fresh meat accompanied by fine local wines. Las Lajas is the last settlement as the road continues to climb. The trees get a little thicker in places before you arrive at Retamar which is 2,220m (7,280ft) high. The valley floor suddenly falls away to form a deep gorge, few trees survive on the steep sides as you skirt the valley, dropping in altitude for the first time. There are good views across the valley but Teide remains invisible beyond the high escarpments of Retamar. As you round the bend the view is breathtaking; Teide and the old peak stand before you framed by the high cliffs of Boca de Tauce. After about 30km (18½ miles) and a climb that is never boring, you meet the Chio road at Boca de Tauce.

The Route from the West

In contrast to the pattern of the book, rather than head anti-clockwise from Las Americas, the next road described is to the west of Las Americas. The reasons for changing the pattern are simple. The south and west roads join before the volcano is reached, the same is true for the northern and eastern routes. Most visitors to Teide will spend time at the summit, returning to their resort having spent all day exploring, climbing and enjoying the mountain. Rather than return by the same route taken in the morning, it is possible to take the connecting road and not drift too far away from your base.

The western route starts at Chio. Approaching from Tamaimo the road is clearly signposted 'Las Canadas' and lies just beyond the Texaco station (be careful not to take the road to Arguayo). If you are coming from Adeje and through Guia de Isora, rather than continuing on the main road, you can cut the corner by taking the roads through either Chirche and Aripe or through Chiguergue. The former is not signposted and is quite hard to find. As you come through Guia look for the Cepsa station on the corner. Beyond the garage is a chemist and a IFA warehouse. Turn right. If you miss the turning there is ample opportunity to turn round before you leave Guia. If entering Guia from Chio the turning is first on your left. Continue up, way from the main road and turn right. Take the turning on the right, continue up and turn right at the T junction. Take the first turning on the left, beyond the Police Station (*Guardia Civil*). From here it is a case of turning right and then left wherever you want, as all the roads lead in an American-style block system to a road where you can turn left to head up or right to turn down into the town.

By turning left you will soon leave Guia and start climbing. The road is narrow but has recently been resurfaced, it follows the contours of the steep terrain to Aripe and on into Chirche. As you drive through these traditional villages it is worth paying particular attention to the architecture. Here you will see as broad a cross section of styles as anywhere in the island. Particularly noteworthy is the wooden balcony that gives so much character to the old house in Aripe nestling in a quaint *finca* just as the road leaves the village. In Chirche, as you climb the road beyond the village, keep a look out for the strange circles, edged by rocks. These date from the times when donkeys were used to sort the wheat from the chaff. You will often see what look like short wooden surf boards with studs in. Now often no more than wall decorations in restaurants, these were harnessed to the donkey and the farmer then stood on the board and was towed across the crop, crashing the staves of corn and separating the valuable ears from the stalks.

At the T junction with the road between Chio and Teide, turn right for the mountain. Continue on the main road out of Guia towards Chio. Beyond the 'S' bend, the big Cepsa station and a bar, is the turning to Chiguergue (signposted opposite the Co-operative.) As you climb away from the road, look back to enjoy the views. From here the coast is visible from Alcala to Playa Paraíso. At night the neon lights of Las Americas create a faint, sunset-like glow beyond the hills.

Chiguergue is a small but busy village, most inhabitants have land in the vicinity where they grow tomatoes, potatoes, carnations, roses and many other crops. The *fincas* are neat and well-tended, bordered by lava walls, constructed by men whose services are much in demand but whose numbers are dwindling as the more practical breezeblock has taken over. In the gardens of the neat houses oranges, almonds and fig trees compete with cacti in the dry soil, irrigated by an intricate system of canals and pipes. As you enter the village there is a road that will allow you to bypass the winding roads of Chiguergue but you will also miss the opportunity to explore this quaint hamlet. The church and plaza stand at the entrance of the village, it is worth taking time to cross the plaza and from behind the church enjoy views across the *fincas* and water tanks to the coast. The bars are usually open in the evening or for Sunday lunchtimes and you will be made welcome in them. Continue past the church and follow the road up, round and out of the village. At the T junction turn right and head towards Teide.

There are only three places to eat on the road from Chio to Teide.

(Above) Sunset over Tenerife; (Below) A traditional Tenerife farm building at Aripe

The first is just after the turning at Chio onto the mountain road, The next lies just beyond the turning from Chirche, and the last just beyond that; all three serve excellent meals. The Bar de Evora is the first notable landmark after you have taken one of the access routes; all the following distances are given from here.

Beyond the Bar de Evora the scenery is suddenly displayed before you, on the bend the foothills rise in an arc of breathtaking beauty, and there is something to catch the eye in every square metre. On the lower hills almond trees stand out displaying their pink blossom in the early months of the new year, by Easter the leaves are out and in August the crops are ready to gather. Fig tree grows here in abundance, their silver bark in bright contrast to the deep green of their leaves and the black fruit. Higher in the foothills, pines begin to take over, seemingly hanging on vertically to the steep sides of the slopes. Please note that almonds and figs are valuable crops, and while some grow wild and at the side of the road and can be picked, many are cultivated by those who rely on them for their livelihood.

Beyond the last bar the crops stop, and there is little farming. The rugged countryside has been left to fallow, for there is little soil, and the floor of the increasingly dense forest is covered with pine needles, cones and saplings struggling for a foothold under their elders.

As the road climbs the forests give way to lava. After 7km (4½ miles) there is a distinct gap in the forest where a lava flow 'crosses' the road; few trees grow in the lunar-like flow, beyond which the mountains of the west coast are visible and beyond them La Palma and Gomera. Beyond Los Poleos, at 1,482m (4,860ft) is Moñtana Chinyero, at 1,510m (4,950ft). This is the site of the last volcanic eruption in Tenerife which occurred in 1909. The lava flows are now cool and still, the sharp faces of the hills were blown apart by eruption and now reveal the multi-coloured rocks below.

Just before Chinyero is an entrance on the left that allows access to the forest. The track is not recommended for cars but you can park and walk. Those visitors who are feeling energetic should head into the interior and eventually, whatever route you take, you will stand to one side of Chinyero, amid the lava flows and ash thrown out from the mountain. It is a strange, quiet land of few trees and plants, a desert-like landscape of lava and geological upheaval. Just beyond Chinyero, on the main road, the view of Teide is revealed, still partially hidden by the old peak.

After 10½km (6½ miles) there is a *zona recreativa* on the right and again there is a chance to leave the road. About 400m (430yd) past the entrance to the park, look for the solitary tree on the left, behind it is the entrance to a 'cinder' track. Within a few hundred metres you can look across the dust and ash at a superb view of the mountain. Before you is the work of mother nature at her most violent and creative. The black lava, specked with the occasional pine in the arid dust, contrasts with the might of Teide in the background. It is a quiet and haunting place, a wonderful part of Tenerife that so many rush and fail to appreciate.

The Montaña de Cuevacitas gives you another chance to stretch your legs. At 1,800m (5,900ft) the pines are few and far between, with only a few remaining on the upper slopes, taking moisture that collects in the ravines. There is a lay-by just after the group of signs, pull off the road and take the well worn track to the right. After a short walk you reach an entrance to the caves. Whether the Guanches lived here is doubtful as only one cave has an easily used entrance. The caves were formed by the action of water cooling the lava flows and one of them is said to continue as a tunnel to Guia de Isora. The caves provide shelter from the sun and that fact is not lost on the hunters and walkers who use the caves for lunch, though unfortunately some leave their rubbish scattered across the floor of the cave.

You climb gradually until the pines disappear, for the air is getting thinner and the conditions are too harsh for them to survive in great numbers. The straight road lies on the lava fields, to one side are the steep sides of the sunken crater you have entered. Ahead are rock formations that stand like sentries around the National Park, their vertical sides bearing witness to the force with which the volcanoes erupted. To the left is the old peak (Pico Viejo), which last erupted in 1798 and in 3 months spewed over 12 million cubic metres of lava onto the slopes. Today the dark scar is still visible in contrast to the vegetation that has claimed much of the slopes. At the end of the straight the road links with the route from Vilaflor and turns to form a single route towards the base of Teide.

This area is known as Boca de Tauce, *boca* being Spanish for mouth. Both roads from the coast, having climbed to a height of over 2,000m (6,650ft), now join to follow a direct route along the side of the sunken crater. To one side is flat desert, to the other are vertical cliffs. Whatever time you drive along this road the sun's position will highlight different aspects of this area's beauty. In the early morning Teide is lit from the east while the valley floor stays in the shadow. In the evening a red sunset will give Teide a fiery glow, making it look as if it is about to erupt.

Las Cañadas (The Ravines) of Teide are named after the several

Moñtana Chinyero, where vegetation is starting to grow on the ash and lava flows from Tenerife's last volcanic eruption

gorges that are visible in the National Park. They are easy to spot as their lighter colour contrasts with the basic, dark stone of the volcano. All the ravines have names and are different in size and character. Despite giving their name to the area, the ravines are eclipsed in beauty by the rock formations, the sandy plains and of course by the majesty of Teide. At the junction there is a lay-by where the authorities have thoughtfully placed an information board concerning the formation of the area. This explains how lichens and

(Opposite) A cinder track through the Chio zona recreativa

other hardy plants came to inhabit the area after the eruptions and how their actions form the soil on which vegetation grows today. The rocks form strange vertical patterns where the strata was folded and pushed from the horizontal; one peak stands alone, rising steeply from the craggy escarpments.

Just over 2km (1 mile) from the junction of the two southern routes is El Zapato de la Reina (Queen's Shoe or Slipper). Easily identifiable, this rock stands below a series of high cliffs. After 3½km (2½ miles) the plains of Ucanca can be seen on the left, the sand and shale-like surface leading to the Roques de García and some of the most unusual rocks in the park. On the road you pass through the cutting of green rock to emerge high above the plain. There are a number of lay-bys from which to admire the impressive view across the plains to the sheer walls of the crater's edge.

After 6½km (4 miles) you can turn left towards the Roques de García. Look towards the volcano and you may recognise a view that appears in many books and on many postcards. The top-heavy monolith leans as it has for centuries, defying many who remain convinced it is about to fall, while in the background Teide remains timeless and awe-inspiring.

There are a number of walkways laid out through the rock formations and visitors are encouraged not to stray from the path by a series of ropes. Opposite the rocks is the Parador de Turismo. This attractive hotel is one of many state-owned hotels throughout Spain and the Canary Islands offering a high standard of accommodation in traditional surroundings. It may seem surprising to find a swimming pool in the rarified air of the National Park, until you sample it. To lie so close to the sun, with Teide reflecting in the clear water, is an unforgettable experience. Close to the hotel is a small chapel which visitors are able to enter. The road beyond the *parador* follows the flat plain until, after 10km (6 miles), you arrive at the entrance to the *teleferico* (cable car).

The Routes from Orotava and Los Realejos

From Puerto de la Cruz you can approach Teide from the two roads through Los Realejos and La Orotava. As you leave Los Realejos look for the signs to Palo Blanco. Turn left, right and then left again, following the signs to Las Cañadas de Teide. This road will take you through the villages of Palo Blanco, El Viñatico, Brezal and Benijos before joining the main road at El Camino de Chasna. This route is about 10km (6 miles) long and is interesting; the villages are small and often unannounced collections of neat houses in the middle of *fincas*. Vines, oranges and potatoes are the main crops here and you will often see signs offering produce for sale (*Se Vende*). Although there are bargains to be had, you need to speak Spanish to be understood. The road winds up and then down, skirting *fincas* where the soil is a rich brown. Life is slow here and much of the work is done traditionally, so that donkeys, mules and cattle are likely to be seen pulling ploughs.

The road from Orotava is one of the most beautiful on Tenerife. The Orotava valley is one of the island's great beauty spots, acres of green that cover the valley floor to provide a breathtaking spectacle. The pines at higher altitudes contrast vividly against the azure background. As the road climbs it passes through small sheltered villages and you enter El Camino de Chasna after 7km (4½ miles). Below bananas blanket the lower slopes while above them are vines and chestnut trees.

Aguamansa is the last village on the road and is easy to miss in your haste to get to the mountain. Its main attraction lies hidden from the road. There is, however, a main entrance on the bend. Just beyond the bus shelter on the junction, look for the wooden sign by the path, 'Sedero Turístico', indicating a footpath of interest. Follow the path up to a woodland, signposted Bosquete (little copse), and just beyond the copse is the entrance to a trout farm, a surprising attraction and one that is very interesting. Apart from the hatchery pools which teem with fish, there is an information centre which provides excellent maps of the various country walks and tracks.

About 1½km (1 mile) from the bus shelter is a track leading off to the left, signposted La Caldera. After 800m (870yd) you reach a small bar and terrace, and a one way system circles a barbecue area. There are permanent barbecues provided by the forestry authorities and a number of freshwater taps. Wood is provided for your use, all you need to bring is food and drink.

As you follow the road around the one way route, there are two turnings off to the right. While they are not recommended for cars, the walk is only a few kilometres and the terrain is easy going. The first road is signposted to Pedro Gil, and after 2½km (1½ miles) the road forks, the right branch leading to a water mine (*galeria chimoche*). Here water flows from the higher ground and is piped to the coast. The left fork leads to Pedro Gil. From the track there is an excellent view of the sheer cliffs which are called Los Organos (The Organ Pipes). A number of tracks fork off the main route and all are worth exploring. For those with four wheel drive vehicles they are passable

(Above) Boca de Tauce is the meeting place of two coastal roads which skirt the side of Teide (Below) This small chapel is close to the Parador de Turismo and is open to visitors

until they narrow. The second turning on the one way system is a mountain road to Santa Ursula. The dirt track follows the terrain down to the coast emerging above the *autopista*.

As the main road climbs, the views are of the coast and of Teide, although from here the foothills and crater are hidden. Teide's conical shape is uninterrupted, the lava and shale contrasting on the steep sides. About 15½km (9½ miles) after La Caldera the junction with the road from La Laguna is approached. Just beyond is the Centro de Visitante, an information centre which is manned by the Forestry Commission. It provides a wealth of facts concerning the National Park and is well worth a visit.

Across the Island's Backbone

The road across the backbone of the island is one of the least travelled routes to Teide and yet it is one of the most interesting and provides excellent views. You can travel from La Laguna or Güimar to join the road that leads to the National Park. Leaving the northern *autopista* at Junction 6, you travel alongside the old airport and into the countryside. The climb away from the plain on which the airport is situated is gradual, a tree-lined road cutting through agricultural land where wheat and maize are grown alongside potatoes and the ever-present vines. The route begins to climb in earnest, and the views open up below. To the south Santa Cruz can be seen beyond the terraces and *fincas* in the foreground.

As you enter La Esperanza you will approach a crossroads. Go left and you will return to Llano de Moro, turn right and the road descends to Tacoronte. **La Esperanza** is a most delightful settlement; hidden amongst the trees are a number of large houses and there are numerous restaurants. The closeness to Santa Cruz means that many of the city dwellers come here to eat, especially on Sundays and fiestas.

Beyond La Esperanza there are three options to continue your journey; south (via the route described on pages 55), north (to Tacoronte), or west towards the mountain. The last route is the one taken here. On leaving La Esperanza is the entrance to the Zona Recreativa de Las Raices. It was here that modern Spanish history was changed with the plotting of Franco and his Generals, who met here to finalise plans that led Spain into the Civil War. The only reminder of these troubled times is a plain obelisk among the trees.

Beyond the park the climb begins, 1½km (1 mile) after the entrance to Las Raices is Montana Grande at 1,200m (4,000ft), from the lay-by the views are of La Matanza in the west and Punta Hidalgo in the east. Throughout the route you will notice tracks leading off the main road. Many of these tracks are passable by car and it is surprising just what varied and interesting views can be found beyond the tarmac. Occasionally you will notice rustic wooden signs, often marked *sin salida* and giving the name of a *mirador* or point of interest. These are too numerous to list individually but it is worth choosing one or two tracks to explore. Many are passable in the car and will always reward you with good views across the countryside.

Almost 1km (½ mile) past the *mirador* at Montana Grande are tracks leading to the mountain itself, and a few kilometres later the views open up as the slopes drop steeply from the roadside. As you pass 1,400m (4,600ft) pines close in again, though the panoramas below can be seen through the less dense parts of the forest. About 2½km (1½ mile) after the Mirador del Viento is an unnamed viewpoint affording spectacular views down to the sea, and a little after that at 1,600m (5,250ft) you pass through an area called El Diablo (The Devil). This area seems strangely named as the ferns, grass, gorse and other greenery make it very peaceful indeed. The junction to Arafo can be seen just beyond here.

Let us leave the high road briefly to describe the route from Arafo and Güimar. This can be reached from either Junction 10 or 11 on the southern *autopista*. By taking the road to La Hidalga and turning left at the T junction you meet the road leaving Güimar for Arafo. The junction is a crossroads, and the road to the mountains is signposted La Esperanza.

Arafo is an agricultural community, it is approached from the same junction, where it is also signposted. The settlement is spread out across the slopes. As you enter the one way system you pass the large and attractive church, around which the commercial premises are centred. Beyond the town a number of tracks lead to small farming communities. The climbs are steep and the roads leave a lot to be desired, so it is far better to park in the centre and perhaps enjoy a refreshing drink in a pavement bar.

Arafo is famous throughout the Canaries for its wine, so it is not surprising to see vines clinging to virtually every *finca* wall as you start the climb away from the town and to La Esperanza. After just over ½km (¼ mile) there is another entrance into Arafo, beyond which the road begins to climb in earnest. The houses and homesteads become more spread out as the road twists and turns over *barrancos* that form part of the beautiful scenery. This route is one of the most attractive roads in Tenerife and yet there are only two restaurants and rarely a car, other than those of the locals. After about 3km (2 miles) is a railway track. Under the bridge is a water mine, a gallery from which pure mountain water is drawn, and the tracks are for the carts that bring the rubble from the mountain.

As the road climbs there are good views looking across the rooftops of Arafo and Güimar — the coastline can be seen in the distance. Vines are everywhere, the *fincas* of crops are protected by stone walls on which there are vines, these hang heavy in July and August with their valuable crop. The climb towards the mountains continues until the last of the vines disappear. Pine trees are already in evidence after 5km (3 miles), and a little later the *fincas* give way to pines. As you ascend, the sheer cliffs in the east become easier to discern as the pine trees rise from their near vertical sides. After 7km (4½ miles) there is a sharp bend in the road from which you can look down on the panoramas of the *fincas*, villages and beyond to the coast. From this height, and particularly in summer, you may find the coast seems distorted in the heat haze that rises from the terrain. In the winter months you may already be above the clouds, looking down on a sea of white.

As the pines thicken, the remaining land is arid and barren, although you may see deserted homesteads. Working this land was never easy and some have succumbed to the advance of tourism and industry below. As you pass the 13½km (8½ miles) point, the pines are more numerous, though on the lower slopes they do not grow very high and you will still find views through the copses. While conifers dominate the plantlife, there are still trees and plants competing for space and moisture. The mimosa tree is spectacular and when in flower in the summer it produces a yellow ball of colour which contrasts with the green and brown of the countryside.

For the next 2km (1 mile) the road is flanked by sheer walls of colourful strata. On these cliffs pines dig deep with their roots in search for water, which at times disturbs the structure and rock falls are common. After 16½km (10 miles) the gradient eases and you find yourself driving along an almost straight road hemmed in by the now dense forests. After 18km (11 miles) you meet the junction of the Teide-La Laguna road.

The route to and from Arafo is one that shows off Tenerife's spectacular scenery to good advantage and it is surprisingly quiet. In a small area there are sheer cliffs, rolling countryside, arid and then productive land. The flora along the way adds colour to the landscape, regardless of the season.

While many views can be enjoyed from the road, *miradors* provide stopping points just off the main route. One such place is the Mirador de la Cumbre, situated off to the right, 2½km (1½ miles) after the junction. The track leads 800m (870yd) to a small car park surrounded by a low lava wall. In the distance is a panoramic view of the Orotava valley and beyond. This *mirador* is often deserted, so that you can stand alone and watch birds of prey capture the thermals and soar.

Along the route are a number of rustic signs announcing firebreaks (*cortafuegos*), many of which are little more than wide tracks difficult to navigate in a car. Just over 1km (½ mile) after the *mirador* is one such firebreak, signposted 'Al cortafuego, sin salida 987m'. This track is passable by car and leads to a small turning circle. Again the outlook is spectacular. Soon after the firebreak you reach 2,000m (6,560ft) above sea level.

At **Ayosa** there is so much to see that it is difficult to know where to point the camera. Trees cling to the sides of the gorge, while below Aguamansa nestles in the distance, a scene of peaceful, serene beauty. Having climbed 2km (1 mile) above sea level, you drop down 20m (65ft) to reach La Crucita (The Small Cross). Pull over into the lay-by where you can enjoy the views north and south. To the south is a deep valley at the end of which lies Güimar. Trees adhere to its steep sides, green against the rust brown of the earth and rocks. Northwards the land falls away towards the coast, just visible in the distance. With the sun behind you the terrain shows its spectrum of colour, just waiting to be captured on film.

After La Crucita the countryside quickly changes. The trees thin out as the climb starts in earnest. The landscape resembles a lunar surface of ash and volcanic debris. The road cuts through the Montaña de Negrita (Black Mountain), with Montañas Roja (Red) and Limon (Lemon). They certainly live up to their names, forming a kaleidoscope of colour in the rock. About 2km (1 mile) from La Crucita the road curves through a corridor showing the strata of rock in purple, orange, crimson, grey and black. The plains to each side of the road are almost devoid of life, evidence of the harsh weather conditions that prevail at this height. If you have chosen a day of poor weather for your journey you may now be above the clouds, the coast and valleys hidden under a sea of cloud. Occasionally the clouds skirt the plains, and wisps of mist roll along in the wind, creating a fascinating and eerie effect. Teide rises closer in the distance, and from Izana, at 2,386m (7,826ft), details of the slopes can be picked out.

During the climb you may have noticed the futuristic buildings that appear from behind the hills and mountains. The Izaña Observa-

The peak of Teide seen from Izaña Observatory

The volcanic peak of Teide

❋ tory looks as if it was constructed for the set of a James Bond film and yet, surprisingly, the tall white towers and buildings do not spoil the panorama. Above the clouds in the pure thin air, astronomers, meteorologists and other scientists look skyward through the optical telescopes. This observatory is an important part of the world's research into space and weather systems.

Now you are well above 2,000m (6,550ft) and still climbing towards the base of Teide, the entire mountain is in view from base to summit. Few remain unimpressed with the volcano, though there is much to see before hurrying to the cable car (*teleferico*). Six kilometres (4 miles) past the observatory entrance you come to the junction with the Orotava road. Turn left and within a few minutes you enter the National Park proper.

The road to the teleferico provides many views that seem unearthly. The landscape is unique, with high-sided cliffs rising from the lunarlike basin below. It is strange to find a hamlet at this height and at so remote a place. **El Portillo** is a centre for the various authorities that service the park, including the Mountain Rescue and Cruz Roja (Red Cross). Around their quarters are a number of bars and restaurants, one of which boasts a swimming pool.

THE FINAL STRETCH TO TEIDE

Along the route are a number of lay-bys from where you can walk a short distance off the road to enjoy the views below. One example is the Mirador de San Jose reached after 6½km (4 miles). Here the ground is white with pumice and the rocks are shades of orange, green and pale yellow. Behind is Teide, the slopes now easily discerned; the grey, rust and black of the lava creating a spectrum of shades that seem to change as the sun travels across her slopes. Just under 2km (1 mile) beyond is the entrance to Montaña Blanca. A track leads up from the road to the summit but is only passable in four wheel drive vehicles. The track has fallen into a state of disrepair — visitors to Teide leave behind many reminders of their visit across the walkways and tracks including broken glass, cigarette packets and other rubbish, sadly spoiling the beauty of this area for others. The *teleferico* (cable car) entrance is nearly 11km (7 miles) from the junctions of the La Laguna and Orotava roads.

The National Park of Tenerife: Las Cañadas

In common with many National Parks worldwide, Las Cañadas is controlled by the government and its agencies. Understandably, Tenerife sees its National Park as a special place, so there are frequent patrols of the roads and places of interest and fines for any transgression of the rules. Most of the regulations are a question of common sense. Leaving litter and rubbish is perhaps the most common offence and one that spoils the area more than anything else. In addition, the fauna and flora are protected and it is not permitted to pick plants whole or otherwise. Many of the tracks that lead off the main road are not open to the public, but are for the use of scientists and other government bodies engaged in research. Yet, despite warning signs, litter bins, patrols and other preventative measures, some visitors to the National Park act irresponsibly. Las Cañadas has stood in mute testimony for centuries, it will remain silent and seemingly unaware of your passing, do not spoil it for future visitors.

TEIDE

The centre of the park is dominated by Teide. It seems that most visitors to Tenerife wish to climb to the top. As a consequence, almost every day of the year thousands of tourists arrive by coach and car to take the *teleferico* ride to just below the summit. There are inevitably queues as the two cable cars carry thirty-three people and take 8 minutes to travel up to the disembarking point below the summit. It is a good idea to either come very early in the morning or wait until mid-afternoon. By then the crowds delivered by the coaches will have departed. At the top of the cable car is a refuge or bar. Here one can enjoy the delights of *lumumba*, a brandy-laced chocolate drink.

In winter the footpath to the summit is kept clear of snow and ice. Straying from it at anytime of year is foolish and also forbidden. A video is often shown to those waiting for the cable car which illustrates and explains the rules governing the mountain, the most strictly enforced of these being the protection of the flora and the rock. In addition, those with heart conditions are advised not to climb, at this altitude the oxygen is rare and breathing can be a laborious matter for even the fittest.

Depending on the weather, the views appear either endless or are swathed in a magical, floating sea of cloud. Vent holes still steam around the crater; they are hot but you can place a hand in for long enough to allow the sulphur to coat the hairs on your arm.

Additional Information

Places of Interest

Aguamansa Trout Farm
Road from Orotava to Teide.
A working trout farm where fresh

trout is available for purchase. Also an aviary and bird sanctuary.
Open: daily from 10am-3pm.
☎ 33 07 01

Even in winter you can climb the path to the summit of Teide

Tenerife has sun, sea, sand — and even snow

Tenerife Fact File

Accommodation

If you have arrived in Tenerife without pre-arranged accommodation then your first task is to find somewhere to stay. In high season this may prove difficult. There are no youth hostels and few campsites. There are, however, pensions which are guesthouses where facilities may be limited but where you will find clean accommodation.

In addition, there are hotels and apartments. The star system is similar to the rest of the world, the more stars the better and probably more expensive the accommodation. A 'key' system is used for apartment complexes. As a general guide, two keys will provide a reasonable apartment with private bath and in a complex with a pool. The resort's Tourism Office will have details.

Basic Things to Pack

Camera Equipment
Ensure that you have film and batteries — while both are freely available they can be expensive. Take care when loading film in the sun and never expose your camera to direct heat or leave them in the car. Developing services are widely available but not all of them offer good quality services.

Clothes
Depending on the time of year, you need to bring mainly summer clothes. However, if you intend to visit the mountain region in winter, a jumper or anorak are needed, as well as a pair of stout shoes.

Food

Tenerife has a number of supermarkets in the resorts that will offer many brand names you will be familiar with but they are often very expensive.

Sun Cream

Visitors should be aware that the sun is very strong — even on overcast days you can get burnt — so a high factor sun cream is advisable as well as a hat in summer. Extra care should be taken to protect children.

Beaches

Tenerife is not renowned for its beaches, those that are natural have black sand or a off golden-grey. Do not let this put you off, black sand is not very different from yellow sand, apart from the fact it gets very hot and obviously shows up more on your skin. There are a number of artificial beaches, notably Playa de las Americas and Las Teresitas.

Books and Maps

For those interested in aspects of Canarian history and folklore a number of books can provide further reading; many bookshops stock English language versions.

There are a variety of maps available and free ones are often given with car hire. The Bravo Alonso map is particularly good but the best is probably the Firestone map.

Churches and Other Religious Buildings

In almost every village there is a church, many will be closed except on days when services are held. The religion of the island is Catholic and you will be welcome to attend any service. The major towns keep their churches open, when visiting please show due respect and make sure you dress appropriately, even when rules are not displayed (see Dress Regulations).

Climate

Tenerife enjoys a very mild climate with the temperature rarely falling below 18 °C or rising above 25 °C. However, in July and August the heat can be considerable, particularly away from the sea breezes. The sun can burn easily and protection is essential.

In winter the weather in the evenings is cooler but often a light jumper will suffice. If you travel up to the mountain areas in winter take warm clothing.

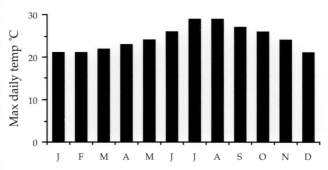

Weather Information: Tenerife

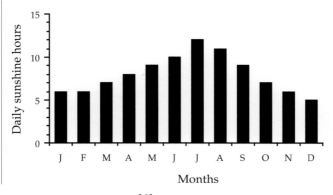

Months

Codes of Behaviour

Fire is a major hazard in Tenerife. Throwing cigarette ends from car windows is an offence for which you can be fined. If you are planning a barbecue use the official and prepared sites and under no circumstances light fires in the forests or green areas. You are not only endangering lives and the islands beauty but laying yourself open to very heavy punishments.

When you leave the island your litter stays. Throughout the island there are bins for rubbish, please use them.

While much of the island is open to the public, there are private lands that should be respected, fences and gates are there for a reason.

In villages and the more remote areas of the island you may find yourself the subject of close but polite scrutiny. If you are walking around a small community where everyone knows each other you are bound to be noticed. The Canarians are renowned for their hospitality and many will wish you *buenas*, an informal hello.

In many of the more isolated villages you may feel uncomfortable if you enter the local bar, but there is no need to. While the bar is often the focus of village life, it is a business and they will welcome your trade. Unfortunately, many bar owners see tourists as fair game to hike up prices. If you feel you are being overcharged there is, by law, a price list in every bar and restaurant that bears a stamp issued by the relevant authority. In addition, a complaints book (*libro de reclamaciones*) is available and you may write your complaint in your native tongue.

Many of the beaches mentioned will not have facilities. While red flags are used at the more popular resorts, they are often not available at the remote beaches, so use your judgement as to the safety of the sea. Make sure that you have food and drink with you and take your litter home.

Common sense should dictate your behaviour. You are a guest in Tenerife, accept this as a guideline and you should not fall foul of either the locals or the police.

Currency and Credit Cards

The Spanish peseta is the currency used and denominations are as follows; 1, 5, 10, 25, 50, 100, 200 and 500 peseta coins. The Spanish are always changing the designs and shapes of their coinage. The old 5 pesetas is being phased out to be replaced by a small gold coin of which there are several versions. The 25 is now a gold coloured coin with a hole in and the 50 a rather strange silver coloured coin. The 500 peseta note has now been totally replaced with a large gold coloured coin and the 100 peseta coin newly issued with "100" written on the face. The latter is certainly less confusing for travellers, previously the word "cien" was the only indication of the value.

All the notes have now been redesigned but the original designs continue in circulation and are valid currency. The colours are the best guidelines, green for 1,000 ptas, red for 2,000, brown for 5,000 and blue for 10,000 ptas. The new notes also have Braille signs for the visually handicapped. In addition to cash, many places, particularly restaurants, accept major credit cards and some allow you to pay by travellers cheques. If you are travelling away from the resorts expect to pay in cash.

Eurocheques and travellers cheques can be cashed at banks and exchange bureaux and many credit cards can be used to obtain cash from banks. There is a limit of 25,000 pesetas per eurocheque. Automatic exchange machines have been introduced to a number of resorts. The current exchange rate is displayed on these.

To pay by any other method than cash you may be asked to produce your passport, this is to prevent fraud. At banks and exchange bureaux you will be asked for your passport and details of where you are staying. Banks often provide the best rate of exchange and there is no limit to the amount you may bring into Spain.

Credit Card Information
American Express ☎ 91 5720303
Eurocard ☎ 91 5196000
Visa/Mastercard ☎ 91 5192100

Cycling and Cycle Hire

Travelling by bicycle is a delightful way to view Tenerife. Some hotels offer cycle hire and there is a specialist shop in El Trebol on the Costa de Silencio. Other shops are beginning to appear in the resorts.

Disabled Visitors

There are no specific facilities or allowances for the disabled. A person in a wheelchair may find some of the town centres full of steps and the pavements too narrow. A notable exception is Los Cristianos where many of the streets are specifically designed for the disabled and there are plenty of ramps for wheelchairs. The Canarians are courteous and will make every effort to help you. Hotels and apartments usually have lifts and doors in such establishments are increasingly being made wide enough to accommodate the needs of the disabled.

Distances

The distances given are by the most direct route. Leave plenty of time for your journey. If you have a specific destination the *autopistas* (motorways) can provide quick but less scenic routes. In summer allow for a few stops, travelling in a car can be tiring and can leave you too exhausted to enjoy the day.

Dress Regulations

You may not be permitted into churches, museums and other national buildings unless you are dressed properly. Shorts and swimsuits are not permitted. In addition, while topless bathing and sunbathing is acceptable at hotels and on beaches, it is not an accepted mode of dress in public places such as bars, nor while walking around. Some beaches are unofficially nudist beaches but naturism on public beaches is not permitted.

Electric Current

Voltage in Tenerife is 220 A/C. Two pin plugs are used so remember to bring an adaptor if you intend to use British or non-standard electrical appliances. The service is often subject to power cuts but most hotels etc have generators.

Entertainment

Tenerife has such a variety of things to do that you will be spoilt for choice. In the resorts everything from jeep and donkey safaris to parascending and waterskiing will be offered. Beyond the resorts, there are specialist clubs and attractions. Excursions are also offered by many hotels and tour operators. In addition, many hotels will have nightly entertainment, and many welcome non-residents.

Fishing

Fishing from the seashore can be enjoyed without any permit being required. There are fishing trips offered in many resorts and recently game fishing has become popular, with marlin, tuna and swordfish abundant in the waters. A tour operator or travel agent will be able to advise.

Health Care

Under EEC regulations an E111 form should provide treatment for UK residents while in the Canary Islands. However, this can often lead to delays and bureaucratic hassle so it is better to have your own private health insurance. American visitors should check they are adequately covered by their health insurance.

The National Health service is very stretched and for minor complaints there is a private system. In the event of accidents and major illness the ambulance service is provided by the Spanish Red Cross and some private companies.

The standard of care in the hospitals is first class. There are major hospitals in Santa Cruz, Orotava, Playa de las Americas and Los Cristianos. In addition, many towns have a medical facility that can provide first aid or treatment. Many doctors speak some English and there are some English doctors on the island. If you or a member of your party are admitted to hospital it is important you provide details of the insurance policy you have or show the E111 form as soon as possible. Equally, if you have any allergies, notify someone as soon as you are admitted.

In all the major tourist resorts and in many towns there are chemists which are open during normal shopping hours. An emergency service is often provided by one in a given area. This information should be available at any hotel reception. However, night calls are often limited to those with a prescription. Chemists have a green cross outside their premises and are called *farmacias*. Brand names that are familiar at home are often available and are not too expensive.

Ambulances have no specific emergency number. The number is usually given in the blue square on the information sheet in the public telephones. If it is not, call 003 and ask the operator. Some of the main numbers are listed below. If a telephone directory is available you will find that the green section at the front has many useful numbers.

Phone Numbers for Ambulances
Santa Cruz ☎ 28 18 00
Icod ☎ 81 01 17
La Laguna ☎ 25 96 26
La Orotava ☎ 33 18 95
Las Americas ☎ 780759
Las Galletas ☎ 785628
Puerto/Cruz ☎ 38 38 12
Los Realejos ☎ 34 12 48
Los Cristianos ☎ 79 05 05
Guia de Isora ☎ 85 08 35
Santiago del Teide ☎ 867318

Hospitals
The ambulance will take you to the nearest hospital that is available and able to treat your complaint. Many are private and will only treat you if you have private medical insurance. It is therefore important to have the relevant documents.

Pharmacy
24 hours ☎ 282424

How to Get There

By Air

Tenerife and the other Canary Islands are surprisingly accessible from Africa and, of course, mainland Spain. However, many visitors arrive from further afield by air.

Scheduled and charter services are frequent and any reputable travel agent will advise you. There are frequent connections with the mainland and Las Palmas, and Gran Canaria has frequent connections with West Africa. The inter-island air service is well used, so booking in advance is advisable. Scheduled services operate both from Great Britain and the USA and in high season you can fly direct.

Airports

Tenerife has two airports. The northern and oldest airport is now used almost exclusively by the inter-island services.

Los Rodeos (Tenerife North)

Just west of Santa Cruz on the northern *autopista* (☎ 25 79 40)

Reina Sofia (Tenerife South)

Just east of the Costa del Silencio on the southern motorway. (☎ 77 00 50)

Flight enquiries ☎ 771375

From both airports there are frequent bus services to the capital and resorts.

By Sea

There are frequent connections with Cádiz by car ferry. Boats, many of them car ferries, also ply between the islands. Recently a jet foil service has been introduced between Tenerife and Las Palmas. Ideal for a day trip, the service runs from the dock at Santa Cruz. Tenerife is linked to Gomera by car ferry and jet foil, both of which leave Los Cristianos.

Transmediterranea ☎ 28 78 50

Ferry Gomera ☎ 21 90 33

Language and Spelling

Anyone who has learnt Spanish elsewhere will be able to make themselves understood, but is likely to be confused at the Canarian tongue. It is more like South American Spanish, with 's' often being dropped, even in plurals.

If you pronounce everything as in English you should get by, the alphabet is the same with some exceptions:

'W' does not officially exist although imported words such as whisky are pronounced as such.

LL is pronounced Y so LlAMA becomes YAMA

CH is pronounced as in English, although there are exceptions. Each word should be taken as seen and pronounced accordingly.

Accents: The Spanish have a system of accents similar to the French, the emphasis being placed on the letter concerned. In addition they have a *tilde*, a curly line over an N; this makes the N pronounced in España as ESPANUH rather than ESPANNER.

Laws for Children

The Canarians adore children and there are few restrictions, apart from in places offering adult entertainment. Children may enter bars unless the owner has placed his own regulations.

Motoring

Roads and Road Signs

The roads in Tenerife vary enormously, you are just as likely to encounter a pot hole on a main road as a country lane. With the exception of the *autopista* (motorway) that joins Santa Cruz to Puerto de la Cruz in the north and the southern section that at present is being extended beyond the airport, there are no dual carriageways. The round-island road is narrow and twisting at times. Generally the roads are adequate and, providing you are in no desperate hurry, they suffice. There are a number of well-equipped picnic areas by the side of the road which also provide space where children can play.

Road signs and markings differ little from those found in Europe. The major difference is the use of white lines and the increasing construction of off-road 'roundabouts' used when turning onto or leaving the main road. A single continuous white line means no overtaking.

To turn left off the main road, leave the road to the right and swing left to stop and give way to traffic continuing on the main road. Give way to traffic right and left and cross when it is safe to do so. To turn left onto the main road, drive across the road as if going straight on and then swing left to give way to traffic coming from the left, using the road as a filter.

Overtaking is probably the most hazardous operation, particularly in a small car. Many lorries and buses will indicate right when in their opinion it is safe for you to overtake. Remember that the onus is on you, so use your own discretion; sounding the horn is an acceptable method of thanking them. The lorry and bus drivers are among the most experienced on the island and when they indicate left in order to tell you that it is unwise to overtake, heed their advice.

Speed limits are there for a reason and are vigorously and strictly enforced by the local police — if the limit is 60kph (37mph) and you are caught doing 61kph (38mph), you are liable to prosecution. The speed limit in a built up area is usually 40kph (25mph) but this can vary. The speed limit on a motorway is 120kph (75mph). Seatbelts are only compulsory outside towns and crash helmets must be worn when riding on a motorbike.

Drinking and Driving
The police in Tenerife have recently started random breathtests. There is a limit similar to the British maximum and prosecution can lead to fines and disqualification. If you are caught drinking and driving, not only are you putting your life and the lives of others at risk but you are laying yourself open to costly fines. Tourists are not exempt from the full force of the law. If you are arrested for whatever reason, ask for a lawyer and inform your consul.

Fuel
There are plenty of filling stations on the island and fuel is relatively inexpensive but you will almost certainly not be able to pay with a credit card.

Hiring a Car

The hiring of transport is something many holidaymakers have experience in. Individual companies will not be recommended but the following advice is offered.

Choose a car that will fit your group most comfortably. The cheapest and smallest option is not always the best. In addition, cars are licensed to carry a maximum number of passengers. Overloading is dangerous and can lead to problems with the company and authorities.

Make sure that all those who wish to drive are on the hire contract. It is a good idea to have at least two drivers named if possible. Before signing the contract read the small print regarding insurance and accidents etc.

Ensure that you are familiar with the car controls. Check the location of the spare tyre, jack and wheel spanner. Again, if in doubt, ask.

It is important to check that the car is in good condition. Hire cars in Tenerife are generally well-maintained. Check the tyres and lights. As in the United Kingdom and the USA, the driver as well as the owner can be prosecuted for certain offences.

Ensure that you have the hire contract with you in the car and that on the contract or in the car is an emergency number, preferably a 24 hour one.

You are obliged under Spanish law to carry your driving licence with you. As British driving licences carry no photograph, you should also carry your passport, as you may be asked to produce it by the authorities.

If the car is not hired with a full tank make sure that this fact, together with any damage to the vehicle, are noted on the contract. If the company asks for a deposit, that too should be written on the contract. If your hire car breaks down, telephone the agency you hired it from first. Do not call out a breakdown service without the agency's prior approval or you may well have to foot the bill yourself.

Under no circumstances leave valuables in an unattended car.

Things You Will Need

Clothing

Despite the excellent climate that Tenerife enjoys, the weather, particularly in spring and autumn, can be changeable. If you are going up and away from the coast it is essential to take a jumper and if you are visiting Teide in winter or bad weather, an anorak or similar waterproof is advisable.

Water

It is advisable to take a bottle of water with you. It is also possible to buy windscreen shades — these help you to keep cool.

Money

Away from the resorts the establishments that accept cheques and credit cards are less numerous. In addition, always carry a good supply of 25 peseta and 100 peseta coins for the telephone.

Hints for the Journey

It is advisable to have at least an idea of a route before you set out, even if 10 minutes from the hotel you find the spot you want to spend the rest of the day. Allow plenty of time for what you plan to do. The roads are not designed for high speed dashes back to the hotel for dinner or to catch the bus to the evening excursion. It is worth remembering, particularly when driving in a strange land and in a strange car, that tiredness causes accidents. It is advisable to take frequent stops to enjoy the views.

Official Regulations for Entry into Tenerife

A current passport is sufficient to allow a British or American tourist to stay 3 months in Tenerife. Further stays require visas and if you are working the laws are very different. If you lose your passport you should contact the consul of the country of issue. A document will be required from the police which the Consulate will advise on; see Useful Addresses for further details.

Photography

There are few restrictions on photography in Tenerife. Common sense dictates most of the rules. Restrictions are obvious around military installations and at the airport you may find you are asked what you are doing. In some buildings and churches photography is not allowed and signs show this, in many cases the use of video cameras is also banned.

There are some signs showing where the best views can be photographed, these are indicated by a picture of a vintage camera. Not surprisingly, you may find a bar or restaurant placed conveniently for your use. If you are photographing private property, you should ask the owners for their permission.

Picnic Sites and Viewpoints

In Tenerife there are a number of *zona recreativas*. These are state-owned and are free to those wishing to use the facilities. They are all open throughout the year and have facilities such as running water, fuel supplies and public toilets. Although they are provided free, you are controlled in what you can and cannot do. Firewood is provided so the chopping of live trees is strictly prohibited, as is the setting of fires outside of the stonebuilt barbecues. You can spend a very pleasant day here but arrive early, particularly on weekends and fiestas.

A summary of the major parks is as follows:

Las Lajas Above Vilaflor on the road to Teide.
Valle de Contador On the old Guimar-Granadilla road above Arico.
Las Raices On the La Laguna-Teide road, just beyond La Esperanza.
La Caldera Above Aguamansa on the Orotava-Teide road.
La Guancha Above the village of the same name between Los Realejos and Icod.
Arenas Negras On the Icod — San Jose road above San Francisco.
Chio Above Chio and Guia on the Teide road.

In addition, you will see many other parks provided at the roadside. Many have barbecues and water etc laid on.

Police

The Spanish police have earned what is perhaps an unfair reputation for being hard, unhelpful and intolerant. However, the police in Tenerife have a difficult job. Every year millions of tourists descend onto their 'patch' and inevitably some of them cause trouble. Like police throughout the world, the job of the authorities here is to protect property, individuals and uphold the law. Providing you do nothing to upset them, they will prove to be very helpful. Cross them, and you will find they are less than tolerant. There are three police forces in Spain. Broadly, they are as follows:

Policia Nacional
These wear white shirts with blue trousers and are generally responsible for matters involving security of national figures, airports etc, though you will probably see them in the resorts checking identities and permissions to work. They control the Spanish system of identity cards and passports and tourists should have little contact with them.

Guardia Civil
The Guardia wear green uniforms and, among other things, are responsible for major crime investigations, traffic and accident investigations. Like the Policia Nacional, you will see them at airports and government buildings. The Guardia are firm but fair. You are likely to see them catching a speeding motorist one minute and helping a stranded driver the next.

Policia Local
These wear blue uniforms. As their name suggests, they are responsible for local matters. Often unarmed, they control traffic and parking, and act as the enforcement body for the local government. They are also responsible for accidents off the main road, although at major incidents they would enlist the help of the Guardia.

If you need the police feel confident to approach them. Although many speak little or no English, they will help if you explain either by sign language or pigeon Spanish (you will find some Useful Phrases later in the Fact File).

If you are stopped by the police, either at a roadside check or for some offence, offer your driving licence, passport and the car hire document. Unless you have commited an offence, the police will allow you to continue on your way. If you are prosecuted, they can ask for the fine there and then. As a tourist you are obliged to pay it. If you feel that you are innocent you may appeal to the issuing authority. When you pay ensure you receive a receipt.

If you are involved in an accident and are not hurt it is a good idea to ask the police to attend. As in Britain and the United States, they will supervise the exchanging of names and addresses. They will attend accidents resulting in injury but can take time to arrive in the more rural regions. If you feel you are the innocent party in any accident, ask any witnesses for their names and addresses and hand the list to the police. Do not make a statement unless you are confident in Spanish or have a translator.

Post

Post offices are open from 8am to 2pm, Monday to Saturday. They will advise you on the stamp required to ensure delivery. Post boxes are yellow and have the word *Correos* clearly marked, as do the post offices. In major towns and resorts the box is divided — local España and Extranero (Extranero being foreign).

Public Holidays

There are many public holidays and fiestas in Tenerife, the major ones are listed below. In addition, you may find that in one town life stops as the citizens enjoy their local bank holiday, whereas life goes on as normal in a town down the road.

January 1 and 6
March 19
Easter Thursday and Friday

May 1
June 4
August 15
October 12
November 1
December 8 and 25

Should the given date fall on a Sunday, then the Monday is often a working day.

Public Toilets

There are very few public toilets in Tenerife, even in Santa Cruz. Bars provide an alternative and owners accept your entrance without problem. Not all are clean and a supply of toilet paper is a good idea. The waste bin is provided to place soiled paper and sanitary towels, do not flush these down as it results in the system being blocked.

Public Transport

In Tenerife this consists of buses, there are no trains. Although there is a comprehensive road system, the bus service to the outlying areas is non-existent or sporadic. There are bus stops on major routes and these consist of blue and red or green and white circular signs. The main bus stations are Santa Cruz, Puerto de la Cruz, Los Cristianos and Playa de las Americas. In addition, many municipal towns have smaller stations. Although many books will tell you that the translation for bus is *autobus*, in the Canaries it is *guagua*, pronounced 'whow-wer'. There are frequent services from most main stations and the buses are green and white or red and white with the word TITSA written on them. State your destination and offer the fare asked for. You may ask for a return fare by saying *Ida y vuelta*. The fares tend to be inexpensive and you usually pay the driver.

Religion

Catholicism is the main religion in the Canary Islands. There are other religions such as Anglican on the island but their authority is very limited.

Shopping

Away from the resorts most shops keep to the hours of 8 or 9am-1pm and 4-7 or 9pm. In the resorts you may find they stay open all day. Most shops close Saturday afternoons and Sundays.

Although the islands are 'duty free' they may not be as cheap or have bargains as good as first thought. Shop carefully; away from the resorts the selection will not be as good but prices are often more reasonable.

Things to Buy
Lace, including bedspreads, napkins and tablecloths are worth buying. Drink and tobacco are more reasonably priced than in many countries. Local liquor includes banana liquor and *ron miel*, a honey rum.

Sport and Leisure

Many of the resorts will offer an array of sport and leisure activities including parascending, waterskiing and scuba-diving. Tennis, squash and gyms are available in many hotels. Non guests may often use the facilities.

Camping
You may, with prior permission, camp in some of the recreation zones on the mountain. The tourist offices will advise you. In the south there is a permanent site in the Costa del Silencio (☎ 78 59 71/78 51 18)

Climbing
Despite the many rock faces and mountains in Tenerife, climbing is not a popular sport. In the National Park it is expressly forbidden. However, there are many walks on the island where climbers may find some face to challenge them. Be careful, however, many of the faces are of soft rock and crumble easily.

Golf

There are three courses on the island which are of championship standard:

North

Club de Golf El Peñon

Just off the northern motorway at Guamasa

Non-members are welcome weekdays between 9am and 1pm. 18 holes ☎ 25 02 40

South

Golf del Sur and Amarilla Golf Club

Both off southern motorway at the Los Abrigos turning. These clubs are both private and while at present non-members are welcome, it is best to check first. 27 holes.

Golf del Sur ☎ 70 45 55

Amarilla Golf Club. 18 holes ☎ 78 57 77

Horse-riding

Cuadra Los Orovales

Located by the rose garden in Camino Carrasco Puerto de la Cruz

Experienced riders will be welcome here, and there is a donkey for the children.

Further information ☎ 38 39 42 (English spoken)

Amarilla Golf Riding Centre

Beach rides and mountain treks.

☎ 78 57 77 for bookings.

There are donkey sanctuaries at Arafo and Santiago del Teide. Visitors are welcome and donkey rides into the countryside are often organised.

Private Flying

Light aircraft can be hired at Los Rodeos (Tenerife North). For further information phone 25 79 40 and ask for the Aero club. It is not always manned but at weekends the club is very active.

Scuba-diving

A professional school is located in Los Gigantes and there are clubs at Las Galletas. There are daily lessons and trips out to sea. Equipment is provided.

Walking

Tenerife has many walks but many of those in the more

remote places are only reached by car.
Popular walks are:
Barranco del Infierno: Adeje
Igueste and the north-east coast: the Anaga
The northern Anaga around Las Palmas: the Anaga
La Caldera to Santa Ursula: Above Orotava on the Teide road
The Monte de Agua: Above Santiago del Teide / Erjos
Masca Beach: From Masca

Walks in the National Park are sometimes restricted.

However, below the park are a number of well-worn tracks that can provide a pleasing stroll into the interior. There are few maps available at tourist information centres so a good sense of direction is essential. In the park guided walks are available at the Visitor's Centre, just off the El Portillo / Teide road. Walks start at 9am, 11.30am and 1.30pm. An interpreter and guide accompany you and there is no charge. For further information phone 25 64 40 or 25 99 03

Taboo Subjects

The Canarians are easy going and there are few taboo subjects. Close ties with South America mean that the Falklands problem is best not discussed and policies of the Americans in South America are likely to receive a frosty rather than aggressive reception. Football is the main topic in the bars. Support for Tenerife, Real Madrid and Barcelona is fervent and contrary comments, no matter how flippant, are likely to provoke some displeasure. It is unlikely, however, that you will receive a violent answer to your comments.

Conversations about the Civil War are best avoided. The Canarians are a proud race and, regardless of your beliefs, criticising Spain, the islands or the people is likely to arouse resentment.

Taxis

Taxis can be hailed in the normal way. Most are white and, with the exception of those in Santa Cruz, do not have metres;

for this reason you may wish to establish the fare before starting. In any case, drivers are obliged to carry a legal fare chart in the cab. Many can be hired to take you on a trip; state where you wish to go and how long you wish to stay out, and a price will be given. It is not normal to haggle but you can ask to see the approved fares and choose a specific trip.

Telephones

The system in Tenerife is improving, albeit slowly. Telephone boxes are aluminium and glass and can be recognised by the word *teléfono*. In addition, many bars have coin boxes or will allow you to call as they have meters. They accept 5, 25 and 100 peseta coins. For local calls 10 or 25 pesetas will be sufficient, for international calls a minimum of 200 pesetas is required.

The alternative are the official tourist kiosks where your call is metered and you pay afterwards. Major credit cards are often accepted at these. To dial abroad dial 07, await the higher pitched tone and dial 44 for the UK or 1 for the United States, followed by the area or STD code less the first 0, then the number. You will hear the appropriate dialling tone as if you were calling from home. The local dialling tone is an elongated sound, the engaged tone is a higher pitched and short tone.

If dialling any part of Tenerife, Gomera, El Hierro or La Palma no code is necessary. If you are calling any other island 928 should prefix the number. The code for Madrid is 91.

In 1995 the new 061 emergency telephone system will become fully operational. From any telephone you need only dial 061. This will access a central exchange. Speak slowly and give your location and telephone number. As the system develops it is anticipated that English speaking operators will be available.

Useful Telephone Numbers
Police
Headquarters: Santa Cruz
    Emergency 091
    Other 21 25 11

Guardia Civil
    Santa Cruz 64 85 00
    Playa de las Americas 79 14 14
    Puerto de la Cruz 38 35 28

Hospitals
Santa Cruz
    General hospital 64 10 11
La Orotava
    Clinic san Miguel 33 05 50
Puerto de la Cruz
    Clinica Bellvue 38 35 51
    Clinica Tamaragua 38 05 12
Playa de las Americas
    Centros Medico del Sur 79 10 00
    Clinica Las Americas 79 16 00
    Clinica Salus 79 12 53

Fire Brigade
North 33 00 80
South — Las Americas 79 14 14

Time

The Canary Islands are often in line with British time, be it Greenwich Mean Time or British Summer Time. Accordingly, most of Europe, including mainland Spain, are 1 hour ahead. There are a few weeks when this is not the case, in the islands it has been known for Summer Time and Winter Time changes to be some weeks before the remainder of Europe.

Tipping

It is easy to get carried away with tipping. As a general rule, in restaurants and taxis a 10 per cent tip is the most one should give. Do not, however, feel obliged to tip, and if the service received has been excellent, a larger tip is a customary way of showing your satisfaction.

Tourist Offices

Tenerife
Plaza de España (Cabildo Insular)
Santa Cruz
☎ 60 55 92

Many resorts also have a selection of tourist offices.

Spanish Tourist Offices

United Kingdom
57-58 St James' Street
London SW1A 1LD
☎ 071 499 0901

USA
845 N. Michigan Ave
Water Tower Place
Chicago, Il. 60611
☎ (312) 944 0215

665 5th Avenue
New York
NY 10022
☎ (212) 759 8822

Case del Hidalgo
Hypolita and St Georges Street
St Augustine
FL 32084
☎ (904) 829 6460

1 Hallidie Plaza
Suite 801
San Francisco
CA 94102
☎ (415) 346 8100

Fortaleza 367
PO Box 463
San Juan
Puerto Rico
☎ 725 0625

If you telephone or call at these offices you can receive a great deal of information to assist you on your visit. However, if writing, specify the Canary Islands as your destination and not Spain generally.

Translations of Widely Used Words in Tenerife

Mirador — Viewpoint
Playa — Beach
Autopista — Motorway
Barranco — Deep valley
Finca — Plot of land
Museo — Museum
Iglesia — Church
Río — River
Parador — Hotel in a historic building

Useful Addresses

British Consulate
Plaza de Weyler
Santa Cruz
☎ 28 68 63
If you phone out of office hours a recording will give you a number.

American Consul
There is an American Consulate in Las Palmas but it is not permanently staffed, so a direct phone call to the Embassy in Madrid is best.

American Embassy
C/Cerrano 75
28006 Madrid
Madrid, ☎ (91) 577 4000

R.A.C.E. (Automobile Club)
Avda. Anaga
Santa Cruz
☎ 27 07 16

Tourist Office
Edf. Cabildo
Plaza de España
Santa Cruz
☎ 24 22 27

Useful Phrases

In the Restaurant

Can I have the menu?	*La carta por favor?*
Pork chop	*Chuleta de Cerdo*
Chicken	*Pollo (pollyo)*
Veal	*Ternera*
Fish	*Pescado*
Steak (fillet)	*Solomillo*
Steak (entrecot)	*Entrecot*

Chips	*Papas Fritas*
Boiled potatoes	*Papas Canarias*
Water	*Agua*
Wine	*Vino*
Local wine	*Vino de Pais*
Red	*Tinto*
White	*Blanco*
Rosé	*Rosado*
Fizzy drink	*Refresco (most brand names can be used)*
In sauce	*en salsa*
The bill please	*La cuenta por favor*

The Car

Dipped headlights	*Luz de cruce*
Parking	*Aparcamiento*
Give way	*Ceda el paso*
Motorway exit	*Cambio de sentido*
Falling rocks	*Desprendimientos*
Roadworks	*Obras*
Danger	*Peligro*
Lorry exit	*Salida de camiones*
Petrol	*Gasolina*
Full (when filling-up with petrol)	*Lleno*
Oil	*Aceite*
Car repairs	*Taller de automoviles*
Driving licence	*Permiso de conducir*
Car	*Coche*
Insurance	*Seguro*
I want to hire a car	*Quiero alquilar un coche*
For one day	*par un dia*
For one week	*par una semana*

Do you have a?...	*Tiene un?...*
How much is it?	*Cuanto es?*
Is full insurance included?	*Es con seguro completo?*
and personal insurance?	*y seguro personal?*
Explain the controls please	*Por favor, explicarme los aparatos*
Where is the spare tyre?	*Donde es la rueda repuesta?*
I want another car	*Quiero otro coche*
Please put the damage and deposit on the contract	*Por favor, nota el daño y el deposito sobre el contracto*
Is the tank full?	*El tanque esta lleño (yenno)?*
I have had an accident	*He tenido un accidente*
Call the police / ambulance	*Llamen la Policia/una ambulancia*
Where is the petrol station?	*Donde esta la gasolinera?*
Fill the tank please	*Llénelo por favor*
Where am I?	*Donde estoy?*
I've had a breakdown	*Mi coche se ha estropeado*
I am at...	*Estoy en...*
How long will you be?	*Cuanto tardarás?*
Where can I park?	*Donde puedo aparcar?*

Note: Signs indicating roadworks ahead are often poorly positioned and frequently fail to give sufficient advance warning. **Be prepared!**

Shopping

I want to look at...	*Quiero ver...*
Jewellery	*Joyas*
Watches	*Relojes*
Cameras	*Cámeras*
Clothes for...	*Ropas para...*
Children	*Niños*
Shirts	*Camisas*
Skirts	*Faldas*
Trousers	*Pantalones*

Underwear	*Ropa interior*
Swimming costumes	*Bañadores*
Have you anything else?	*Tiene algo más?*
Have you anything cheaper?	*Tiene algo más barato?*
That is expensive	*Eso es muy caro*
I will pay only	*Solo pagaré*
Do you have?	*Usted tiene?*
Film for this camera	*Un rollo para este cámera*
Nappies	*Pañales*
Aspirin	*Aspirina*
Sanitary towels	*Compresas*

General Expressions

Good morning	*Buenos Dias*
Good afternoon	*Buenas Tardes*
Good evening	*Buenas Noches*
Good night	*Buenas Noches*
Hello	*Hola*
Goodbye	*Adiós*
See you later	*Hasta luego*
Please	*Por favor*
Thank you	*Gracias*
Mineral water	*Agua sin gas (still)*
	Agua con gas (fizzy)
Where is?	*Donde esta?*
I would like	*Quisiera*
Left/right	*Izquierda/derecha*
Big/small	*Grande/pequeño (a)*
Hot/cold	*Caliente/frio*
Old/new	*Viejo/nuevo*
I do not understand	*No comprendo*
Do you speak English?	*Habla usted Inglés?*
Help!	*Socorro!*

Call a doctor	*Llamen un medico*
What time is it?	*Qué hora es?*
The bank	*El banco*
The post office	*El correos*
A telephone	*Un teléfono*
The beach	*La playa*
The tourist office	*La oficina de turismo*
The dentist	*La dentista*
The car	*El coche*
I have lost…	*He perdido…*
My passport	*Mi pasaporte*
My wallet	*Mi cartera*
My handbag	*Mi bolso*
My children	*Mis niños*
My husband / wife	*Mi Marido/mujer*
My flight tickets	*Mis billetes de vuelo*
Can I change money here?	*Puedo cambiar dinero aqui?*
I have travellers cheques / cash	*Tengo cheques de viaje/billetes*
Do you accept…?	*Acepta usted…?*
Credit cards	*Tarjetas de credito*
What is the exchange rate?	*De que la divisa para esterlina?* (sterling, *dolares, dollars*)
Stamps	*Sellos*

Numbers

One	*Uno*
Two	*Dos*
Three	*Tres*
Four	*Cuatro*
Five	*Cinco*
Six	*Seis*
Seven	*Seite*

Eight	*Ocho*
Nine	*Nueve*
Ten	*Diez*
Eleven	*Once*
Twelve	*Doce*
Thirteen	*Trece*
Fourteen	*Catorce*
Fifteen	*Quince*
Sixteen	*Dieciseis*
Seventeen	*Diecisiete*
Eighteen	*Dieciocho*
Nineteen	*Diecinueve*
Twenty	*Viente*
Thirty	*Treinta*
Fourty	*Cuarenta*
Fifty	*Cincuenta*
Sixty	*Sesenta*
Seventy	*Setenta*
Eighty	*Ochenta*
Ninety	*Noventa*
One hundred	*Cien*
Two hundred	*Doscientos*
Twenty-one	*Vientiuno*
Sixty-six	*Sesenta y seis*
Eighty-two	*Ochenta y dos*

INDEX